Meeting Sophie

Meeting Sophie

A Memoir of Adoption

Nancy McCabe

University of Missouri Press   *Columbia and London*

俔工丂琴

Copyright © 2003 by
The Curators of the University of Missouri
University of Missouri Press, Columbia, Missouri 65201
Printed and bound in the United States of America
All rights reserved
5   4   3   2   07

Library of Congress Cataloging-in-Publication Data

McCabe, Nancy, 1962–
    Meeting Sophie : a memoir of adoption / Nancy McCabe.
    p. cm.
ISBN 0-8262-1495-9 (alk. paper)
    1. Adoption—China.   2. Intercountry adoption—China.
3. Intercountry adoption—United States.   4. Single mothers—
United States.   5. Adoptive parents—United States.   I. Title.
HV875.58.C6 M33 2003
362.73'4—dc21
                                                    2003010935

♾™ This paper meets the requirements of the
American National Standard for Permanence of Paper
for Printed Library Materials, Z39.48, 1984.

Designer: Kristie Lee
Typesetter: The Composing Room of Michigan, Inc.
Printer and binder: The Maple-Vail Book Manufacturing Group
Typefaces: Minion and Helvetica Neue

Photos by Bill McCabe

"In Another Tongue" reprinted from *Prairie Schooner* (fall 2003)
by permission of the University of Nebraska Press.
Copyright 2003 University of Nebraska Press.

Brief portions reprinted from *After the Flashlight Man:
A Memoir of Awakening* (2003) by
permission of Purdue University Press.

Note: Some real names in this book have been changed.

In memory of Bill J. McCabe
1929–1999

and for Sophie, with love

Contents

Acknowledgments

Many people offered invaluable support during the events of this book as well as the writing of it. My social worker, Pat Wheeler, was the kindest, wisest guide I could have found. Members of her international adoption support group and the Feminist Book Club of Clinton, South Carolina, gave me perspective during a long process and gave a warm welcome to Sophie. A special thanks to the Berg and Hatfield families, Grace Yeuell, Anita Gustafson, Ann Moorefield, Janet Henley, and Lynne Simpson. Petra Fiero, Karen Hindhede, and Claudia Routon bolstered me through the ups and downs; Ladette Randolph did likewise and later gave me insightful feedback on this manuscript. I am grateful for the lifelong friendship of Ruth Yoon and her insight on cultural issues. Myrna Nurse's presence in our lives was a great gift during our last year in South Carolina. The Yeuell-Besudens, Gustafsons, and Dutrows provided support and emergency babysitting during our crisis, and I'll never forget the courage and generosity of many students, in particular Doodle Harris. Jodi Bartlett and the Jamison family took spectacular care of Sophie on many occasions as well. A special thanks to my many colleagues at the University of Pittsburgh at Bradford who made our transition effortless and who daily create such a sane, creative, supportive, and stimulating environment. I am especially grateful to Scott and Carys Evans-Corrales and Don Ulin, and I'm very appreciative of the technical assistance of Glenn Melvin and Dennis Siepierski.

Many terrific writers offered helpful critiques on drafts of this manuscript: Stephanie Anagnoson, Thea Atkinson, Debra Cumberland, Walter Cummins, Cara Diaconoff, Sean Doolittle, T. J. Forrester, Susan Henderson, Mary Krawczak, Walter Maroney, Sue O'Neill, Gail Siegel, August Tarrier, Heather Tosteson, Monica von Bayern, Joan Wilking, and Wayne Yang. Avital Gad-Cykman, Season Harper, and Maryanne Stahl also provided useful feedback. Terri Brown-Davidson, Angela Havel, and Richard Lewis were especially perceptive and thorough in their responses.

Anna Smith's good friendship and comments on my work inspired me during the last leg of this project, and my aunt Gena Shipley sustained us with her sage advice and wonderful parties for Sophie. It would take several books to detail the kind acts of my dear friend Sara King and my cousin Jody Shipley and several lifetimes to repay them.

Most of all, I am grateful to my mother and late father, Lucille and Bill McCabe, whose unflagging enthusiasm and practical help made this journey possible, and to my miraculous daughter, Sophie.

Meeting Sophie

Prologue
China, 1999

The baby is screaming again. My baby. I hoist her off the narrow hotel bed—again—and try to cradle her as I rock my torso back and forth in an uncomfortable straight-backed chair.

This baby does not cradle. She doesn't know how to cuddle, to be soothed in anyone's arms. She howls and arches away, squirms and flops, a sixteen-pound fish out of water. I'm not used to holding babies, and she's not used to being held, but when I try to put her down, she wails. My arms feel chafed, raw, and my wrists ache from the hours of straining to hang onto her.

Huge tears pool in her eyes. These tears could break my heart. These screams could break my eardrums.

God, I'm weary. Sometimes it startles me how beautiful this baby is despite the rash that inflames her face, the nick in the corner of her eye where her fingernail caught the skin, sores and scars up and down her arms from her incessant scratching. The beauty of her bright eyes and even features surprises me again and again, as does the sheer power of her small lungs. She has barely rested them in the two days since she was placed in my arms.

Outside the window, many floors below, China is an abstraction. I am too lost in the foreign country of parenthood to focus on the birthplace of this baby. Despite Chinese language classes, when I go outside, indistinct words swirl around me, a womblike roar. In contrast to the stifling heat out there, the hotel is cool and quiet, guards stationed at the doors of the marble-floored and thick-carpeted lobby.

My friend Sara, who taught and traveled in Asia for nearly three years, used to write to me about squat toilets without stalls, Chinese women gaping openly at tampons and pale pubic hair. She told me about rats falling into her bathwater and people blowing their noses on bus floors. She described visiting a zoo containing nothing but a snake, some goldfish, and a house cat.

The letters from Sara and my Lonely Planet tour book may prove to have more depth and flavor than my own experience of China. Sometimes, when I drag my attention away from the baby long enough to look out the window of this immaculate room with plenty of hot water and a western toilet, I'm surprised by the incongruity of the buildings below, their broken and boarded windows yet still the ubiquitous sign of habitation, laundry strung on lines outside them.

For days my ears have been buzzing, my bones heavy with exhaustion. Even before the baby, my group rushed from one tourist attraction to the next, our bus plowing along honking through the May Day crowds that swarmed subways and flooded by on bicycles, carrying children balanced on handlebars or towing platforms loaded with watermelons, live chickens, or stacks of cardboard boxes. We outstripped a wedding procession led by a red car streaming with ribbons and bearing bride-and-groom hood ornaments, passed a bus with three Chinese to a window, faces pressed close to stare at us.

This isn't what I expected of my trip, all this rushing to outrace other vehicles, these occasional distracted glances down from a high-rise hotel. I imagined finding the kind of peace in China I've felt reading Chinese American literature and Chinese philosophy. I would be calmed by the lovely, serene names of buildings at the Forbidden City: the Halls of Supreme Harmony and Earthly Peace, the Palace of Concentrated Beauty and of Peaceful Old Age. I would wander the Temple of Heaven where emperors used to go to pray for a good harvest, anticipating my baby, praying for my own good harvest.

Instead, russet buildings, stone bridges, bamboo-lined roofs, long tiled walkways, and marble terraces barely made an impression on me. I was watching children, thinking, Could I love that one? That one?

And I was obsessing. Normally able to shift my focus from my troubles and find some perspective, this time I couldn't shake them in the face of impending parenthood, which I told myself was surely far more profound than my petty conflicts about my job or the hurt I nursed because I hadn't heard from my parents.

When I met my child, I expected that her presence would shrink my other worries down to size. I had vague pictures of picking tea leaves on a mountainside while she babbled cheerfully in a sling. Contented, fulfilled, I would push her in a stroller along West Lake, soothed by the gentle lapping of water and the misty mountains in the distance, no longer driven by ambition and desire, no longer fearful about the imminent disintegration of my career, which just wouldn't matter anymore.

Instead, I've hauled her from office to office, completing paperwork. Instead, my hearing has started to deteriorate after hours of her high-decibel screaming. I spend my days picking her up to sway her while she screams. The drying laundry that hangs over the mirror and the backs of chairs casts shadows in the fading light, making the hotel room feel like a tent. The sour smell of dirty diapers, the result of relentless diarrhea, penetrates the Ziploc bags in which I've sealed them. Bowls encrusted with rice cereal and bottles opaque with formula residue form their own little cityscape of high rises and squat structures on the windowsill.

Too tired and despairing to go on, I lay the baby on the bed. She bangs stacking cups together and shrieks. Yanking hard at her hair, she struggles to stay awake. Even desperately worn out, her dark little eyes are quick, observant, taking in everything, overstimulated after ten months in an orphanage lacking much to stimulate her.

My cousin is downstairs sending e-mails that my parents don't respond to. I wish she would come back and help me out.

I'm supposed to be part of a new breed of single mothers by choice, women with the resources and desire to raise a child even if marriage is nowhere on the horizon. We are supposed to be economically stable with extensive support networks of family and friends; I'm an imposter by all counts. A few months ago I couldn't resist checking out the now-defunct Sweet Chinese Men website, which promised to match American adoptive single mothers with Chinese husbands. The website proclaimed that we are "the true Ladies Liberty!"

I don't feel like a Lady Liberty. I can't even remember why I wanted to adopt a baby, if I ever knew. In my moments of doubt, I used to believe that in China, the country's landscape and history and architecture and traditions would call forth in me the correspondingly ancient instinct that brought me here, a certainty that becoming a parent is my life's next logical step. Instead, I've just felt like a tourist.

As an English professor, a writer, and a voracious reader, I've spent my life immersed in language, grounded and centered by concrete images; the ability to put experience into words allows me to revel in its richness and make its complexity manageable. It has been the tools of writing—exacting phrases, the connections afforded by metaphors—that have made me feel less alone. And somehow I believed that it was not such a great leap to become a mom, that a child would give me these same gifts, grounding and centering me, offering perspective, connection, and courage. And I, in turn, who have rarely belonged anywhere, could give her a place to belong.

While my baby flails on the bed knocking toys together, I perch beside her. My back no longer just aches, it burns, it feels incapable of holding me up.

My fantasies now are about sleep. I daydream about long, uninterrupted hours of it. Sometimes I imagine being back in my own apartment with my own dishwasher and laundry facilities nearby. And yet whenever I am homesick, my stomach starts knotting up again. Right before I left South Carolina, I baby-proofed my apartment, plugging outlets, hooking plastic locks onto cabinets, rolling up blind cords, gating the stairs. Now, as I plead with my yelling, pounding baby, "Please go to sleep. Just go to sleep," it seems as if I've plugged up my own sources of energy, gated off my own creativity, and locked away my peace and solitude.

The baby regards me silently and then emits a high-pitched shriek. I grit my teeth. It is duty, not yet love, that keeps me patting her, struggling to comfort and calm her.

Everything before today feels like a dream. Even two days ago feels like a dream, the memory of walking in Beijing, through air full of cottony puffs like the shedding of thousands of cottonwood trees, the state tree of my native Kansas. Too restless and anxious to sleep, I walked past the old moat lined with weeping willows, my eyes seeking out the few English signs: the Nightman Disco, a mysterious establishment called "Roly Poly Turtle," a diner labeled "Western Restaurant." Walking, walking through unbearable heat, wishing I could relax, sleep. But whenever I was about to slip into unconsciousness, all the little kernels of worry started exploding like popcorn in my brain.

The night before we left Beijing to meet our babies in Hangzhou, we went to an acrobatic show, all of the parents-to-be in our group vacant-eyed with exhaustion, swaying rather than walking, slumping into red velvet seats. I thought maybe I was hallucinating all the bright costumes, the traditional music, the movements combining martial arts and tumbling and body contortions. I kept dozing off while children stood on their hands, spinning cloth and tables and each other on their feet. I'd start awake to watch them walk across swinging ropes, twirl plates on long poles as casually as if they were holding umbrellas, balance on boards and barrels, build a rickety pyramid of chairs, and climb long tubes while rearranging their bodies into impossible configurations. My dreams were shattered by a table falling and breaking, a plate clattering to the floor. I jerked to consciousness to see the pyramid of chairs become so quivery that the performers gave up on it, hopped down, and signaled for the stage lights to dim.

For the first time in hours, days, maybe weeks, I was free of anxiety: fatigue and serenity felt like the same thing. Each mistake, each falter, seemed purposeful, choreographed and executed to emphasize the precariousness of objects and bodies, the difficulty of equilibrium.

A woman on stage lit candles, recreating a Buddhist ceremony with eerie Tibetan music and a scene of the Himalayas in the background. She hung upside down spinning candles on her feet; darkness fuzzed along the edges of my vision, and I was feverish, shivering from the cold of the mountaintop, burning from the heat of the fire. And in that moment, like a dream, the impossible seemed entirely possible. That people actually built the Great Wall, all that stone that had seemed organic to the mountaintop when I climbed it earlier that day. That a boy rocking on barrels in front of me could defy gravity. That someone was going to hand me a baby and somehow she would be mine.

That feeling has never returned, that confidence flickering in a moment of near-oblivion days ago. I find myself panicking instead, looking at my watch, wondering just how long one child can holler and resist sleep, wondering just how long a day can last.

My cousin has been gone an hour. I've been waiting all that time for the baby to calm down and sleep. I ease down on the bed beside her but she's not used to this, either, and rather than nestling against me, she squirms and screams. She's ten months old, but she can't sit up or roll over. All she can do is toss wildly.

I lay her on my chest. This seems to confuse her. She rolls around a little, then abruptly goes still.

I lift up to investigate.

Her tongue pokes out between her lips, then disappears into her mouth. This new discovery quiets her: she has a tongue.

In the tongue goes, out again. I had a cat once that, after drinking, kept forgetting to put its tongue back in its mouth. Everyone in the household walked around imitating the cat, going about our tasks with our tongues peeping out.

I stick out my tongue at Sophie Qiaoqin. She giggles.

"Where's your tongue?" I ask, and hers worms out obediently, then withdraws.

She flicks it out again. I feel it tickle my chin. She looks surprised again, then pleased with herself;.it's a revelation that her tongue can taste, can lick.

She attacks my chin and my cheeks like a slobbery dog.

I explode with laughter and atop my vibrating chest, she grips my shirt, riding the earthquake of my mirth, then renewing her attack.

And then she is laughing, too, a musical baby laugh.

"Where's your tongue?" I say, and it reappears, and we laugh raucously in that darkening hotel room, the knots in my stomach briefly unraveling. We laugh, we have tongues, we can defy gravity, construct our own wonders: we laugh, mother and daughter for the first time.

South Carolina

1

The first time I saw my niece, other than as a prehistoric creature in an ultrasound photo, she was a month old. My feelings for her leapt out of nowhere, unexpectedly fierce. She weighed five pounds, and her skin was hot and soft as grapes left out in the sun. I lived far away, and I knew I would never ever stop feeling greedy for time with this baby.

At two, learning the words to "Rudolph the Red-Nosed Reindeer," she stared into my eyes with daunting trust and delight. She watched mesmerized as my fingers hopped through "Little Bunny Fufu," and she supplied the rhymes when we read *Madeline* and *Custard the Dragon*. Even when I was with her for that day or two twice a year, I missed her; I knew my brother would never let her come live with me. Someday I was just going to have to have my own baby.

But I worried: what if I had my own child and found I could never love her as much as I loved Sidney?

That was far from the only obstacle. I'd been divorced for eight years. My lethal combination of severe shyness and ever-increasing independence, along with my preference for reading books and writing all night rather than socializing, meant that my prospects for remarriage were dim. I'd spent a lot of time in school, supporting myself but accumulating no savings, and now, in my early thirties, I had yet to launch my career.

A news show that dealt with China adoption took me days to shake off. I had an irrational yearning to board a plane and go beg for one of those babies. At the time, China adoption wasn't open to single people, a fact that helped mitigate my impulses. But I spent a Saturday at the public library reading about routes to becoming a single parent. A few months later, when I happened upon a magazine article about a single woman who adopted from China, that became an option, after all.

That's it, I decide, the same month I accept a teaching job at a college in South Carolina, half a country away from my niece and my native Midwest, even though the school's church connection makes me a little uneasy. But the job market is tight, and this is a job, and I am going to adopt a baby from China.

Right before I move, I drive from Nebraska to Branson, Missouri, for a three-day visit. Three days is my absolute limit for being a nice person. After that I turn short-tempered and irrational, which used to lead Mom to say, in her cheerful long-suffering way, "You can catch more flies with honey than with vinegar." She never said this to my brothers. My dad likes to quote his mother's favorite saying: "If you can't say anything nice, don't say anything at all."

I prefer Alice Roosevelt's version: "If you can't say anything nice, sit by me." And why in the world, I finally ask, would I want to catch flies? Is *that* what my mother dreams for her daughter—to be popular with buzzing, disease-ridden insects?

Deep down, I'm a little worried, though. What if I don't know how to live with anyone anymore?

Whenever I visit, Mom tells me the same stories over and over. She has developed a series of narratives meant to encapsulate each of her children's personalities and approaches to life. My summary goes like this: I am three years old, announcing of my own volition that I want to attend the day-care program offered by the hotel where we are vacationing. Furthermore, I instruct my parents, if they should happen by, they must pretend not to know me.

This is supposed to show my independence—how even at three, I was raring to leave home, how even at three, the spirit that would eventually take me far from home was manifesting itself. My mother's narrative has to it a hypnotic simplicity, erasing any hint of self-doubt or fear of loneliness or broken attachments or painful losses. I am briefly persuaded by this version of myself, given courage by the idea that some mythical reserve of cold-hearted determination will see me through.

The first stop on the tour of my parents' new house in the Missouri Ozarks is Dad's downstairs office. He has hung framed thank-you notes from George Bush for contributions to the Republican party, memorabilia from his navy days, and citations from Boeing Military Aircraft for his work with electronic warfare. The bookshelves are stuffed with Bible commentaries.

For just a second I feel how little I ever belonged in my parents' world, how my loyalties to them and to my own very different world make me often feel like parts of myself are standing on opposite sides of a street, picketing and heckling each other. Maybe this is what draws me to adopt a baby from another culture, believing that somehow we will be able to heal the splits in each other.

Dad's pinched nerve is bothering him again, and he can barely walk. He tap-taps alongside me on my grandpa's old cane, pointing out things: the air filter system that sounds like a bug zapper, the spot behind the deck where he's going to transplant my great-grandmother's forsythia, the place where, when the trees are bare in the winter, you can see all the way down to the lake. The realtor listed the house as a "winterview" rather than "lakeview" property.

"Hear that?" Dad says.

Even through three feet of insulation, I can hear the throbbing of cicadas, swelling so loud I picture as many cicadas as there are leaves in the woods behind the house.

"Those are the seventeen-year locusts," Dad says.

We called a truce on politics a few years ago and now we stick to safe topics: wildlife, vegetation, construction materials, dinner, Sidney.

After dark, the volume of the cicadas rises as if the woods are snoring. In my dreams the sound is thick enough to hold my weight and bear me over the trees.

The sound makes me feel lonely, unrooted. I harbor a childish desire for my parents to stay, ageless, in the house where I grew up in Kansas, leaving it unchanged. Instead, that house now sits empty, and I am getting ready to move halfway across the country to a tenure-track job, something potentially permanent, stable, and settled after twelve years of constantly relocating for another job, another degree. I lie in bed listening to the cicadas and feeling sad about having nowhere to go home to.

In the morning Sidney drags Dad out of bed at sunrise to make her pancakes. She and my brother are living with my parents right now, ever since my sister-in-law abandoned her family. Sidney is three now. "I miss my mom," she says often, sadly, but as she tugs my dad to the kitchen she says confidently, "You'll never leave me, Grandpa."

Like an old man, Dad hobbles along, trying to keep up with her. My heart stalls. How can she possibly understand that my dad will leave us someday? How can I possibly understand that? My dad grew up with all brothers; he had two sons. And then there was me. He had no idea what to do with me. With Sidney, he's had a second chance to get it right, and when I see them together, the miracle of the adoration between them, my childhood wounds shrink. I want my child to have this kind of relationship with him. I want my own second chance.

The last night of my visit, mute with exhaustion at being reduced by my parents' stories, I carry Sidney past the gallery of pictures of us and our ancestors in the family room.

"Who's that?" I point to a picture of me at two, clutching a naked doll with frazzled hair, my own light hair as wild and tangled.

"Sidney," she says.

"No, that's me. Aunt Nancy."

We pause before my dad, aged two, blond and chubby in a long white gown. "Who's this?" I ask.

"Aunt Nancy."

"No, that's Grandpa." I point to a picture of Sidney. "Who's that?"

"Grandpa," she answers.

Sid satisfies any desire I might have for a child who shares my genes, who looks like me. What I long for is a different kind of continuity, to watch a child grow up every day, not just in brief snatches here and there.

Upstairs we crouch for what seems like hours, waiting for the bird to pop out of my great-grandma's cuckoo clock. It burps sometimes, false alarms. Finally, impatient, I force the door and seize the bird's beak until it lets out a strangled cuckoo.

"Again!" Sid yells, and I turn the hands until the wooden bird shoots out.

"Again!" she demands.

I shoot a glance back at Dad in his recliner. Once upon a time he would have ordered me to quit messing with his clock. But he indulges Sidney more than any of us. He just grimaces. I grab the bird again.

"Again," she begs. "Again."

And so it goes on, me yanking at the bird and turning the clock hands, happy to alter time, stop it, whatever she wants.

That night she falls asleep on my lap while we sit listening to music on the sunporch in the dark, overlooking the trees that pulse with the sound of cicadas. The tape player clicks off and the cicadas swell to fill the silence; Sidney's sleeping weight numbs my legs. I imagine my great-grandmother's forsythia blooming below and more cicadas emerging after seventeen years and seasons changing and our cells sloughing off as new ones appear while I sit there, barely breathing, watching my niece sleep.

I've always been a homebody at heart. How have I become such a no-mad, my television in transit during every Summer Olympics, my voter registration switched to a new state every presidential election?

In the living room, the TV drones while my parents page through the newspaper, interrupting each other every few seconds to read items aloud.

"She's asleep," I say. Much as I want to go to bed and read, away from people, inertia sets in the second I perch on the edge of the sectional couch. Mom nudges a pile of newspaper toward me while Dad sighs and reads aloud a quote from a Democratic senator.

"How does he expect small business owners to make a profit?" Mom says.

"I'm thinking about adopting a baby," I blurt out.

Dad lowers his newspaper and peers at me over his reading glasses, and I feel silly about bringing up my vague plan, really nothing more than a pipe dream.

"That's wonderful!" Mom says.

Dad doesn't argue or sigh, which I hope means he's not heavily opposed.

It's just like my parents to take such announcements in stride, without expressing any concern about me being fresh out of school or unmarried. It's not always easy to read my parents' reactions. They often initially appear almost unnaturally accepting of my decisions. They said nothing when, at nineteen, I became engaged to a man I didn't really love, someone who'd pursued me so hard during such a difficult time in my life, it seemed easiest, after a while, to give in. Mom and Dad didn't share their reservations with me, and I didn't let on how shocked I was to find myself married to someone for whom the pursuit had been far more exciting than the capture.

During the five years of my marriage, our finances and our relationship were far too unstable for children ever to be an option. When I separated from my husband, it was months before I told my parents in a letter. People didn't get divorced in my family except in the case of errant wives who abandoned two uncles and their children; it was clearly understood that the marital problems were not the faults of my uncles. But when I chose to end my marriage, my parents took that in stride just like everything else.

Over the last few years, as I finished one degree in Arkansas, taught in Missouri, and went to Nebraska for my Ph.D., I've hinted around that I might have a baby through artificial insemination. Mom always shuddered. It was fun to tease my parents, but I wasn't especially drawn to that route; raising a child was far more important to me than giving birth, and as soon as it occurred to me, the idea of adopting took hold. I have many adopted cousins; I know that to my parents, adoption is commonplace, while reproductive technology—and the notion of an unwed pregnant daughter—would be more alarming. So I fully expect my parents to be relieved by my decision.

But I know that they aren't just relieved, but genuinely pleased, when Mom says promptly and firmly, "Any child of yours will be our grandchild."

Dad gently rocks the sagging chair, letting Mom speak for both of them.

I figure I might as well get everything out in the open. "It probably won't be white," I say. Although some of my relatives have made ignorant comments about Asians, my mother has always told me that she doesn't care about the race of any man I bring home—just as long as he doesn't smoke. So it doesn't surprise me when she replies, "Then we'll have a black grandchild."

"Actually, I'm thinking about China," I say.

"Then we'll have a Chinese grandchild," Mom answers without missing a beat.

I head off to bed with the unfamiliar feeling of being surrounded by unqualified approval. My parents were never, it turned out, thrilled with my marriage. Mom was uneasy when I went back to grad school twice, torn between her reverence for education and her bewilderment, having grown up during the depression, that anyone would willingly be poor for so long.

At least subtly, my parents and I have always been at odds. Once I declared that I was going to join Wicca someday. Years later, Mom accused me of saying such things just to hurt her and Dad, and while I'd never intended to wound them, I had enjoyed goading them, just as I did on the occasions that I've accompanied Mom to church. Gleefully, I've pointed out the minister's slip-ups, like "Christ's death and erection" or "God's impotent power."

"He *said* 'death and resurrection,'" Mom reprimanded me. "He *said* 'God's omnipotent power.'"

Maybe I've always felt a little hostile about my perception of my parents' expectations. Mom laments that she didn't get a daughter like Marie Osmond, a bright, sweet, cheery sort who, despite a divorce and some depressive episodes, is married with children and, according to Mom's magazines, close to her mother.

I've tried for the closeness Mom craves, but she can't remember the names of my friends, changes the subject when I've mentioned dating, and blanks out if I talk about my work. And then she'll say, wistfully, "I wish I knew you better."

"It grieves us that none of you children go to church," she told me in my early twenties, when I was still regularly attending a Bible study group and trying out Episcopal services, Catholic masses, and Quaker meetings, seeking a place that felt right for me. I finally gave up. I wasn't comfortable with any organized religion, and unless I took up quoting Bible verses and asking for prayers on my behalf, I didn't think I was ever going to be religious enough to assuage my mother's grief.

So, washing my face and brushing my teeth after I tell my parents that I'm going to adopt, I bask in their pleasure. I have a full-time job; it's at a church-connected college; I'm going to adopt a baby. I go to sleep believing that I have found a way to reconcile what my parents want for me with my own desires.

As I drive away the next morning, back to Nebraska to wait for the movers, one wayward cicada rides along. At first I mistake it for a fallen leaf on my hood. But when I take off down the road, its wings flap up like a skirt on a windy day, and it clings and clings, holding on fiercely as I pick up speed.

And maybe it's social conditioning, or subtle family pressure, or some ridiculous, erroneous sentimental impulse, or a timeless heartfelt longing for real connections in the world, but I drive off into my new life in South Carolina because it will make possible this child, because the desire to settle down and have a baby just keeps clinging like that determined cicada, keeps singing through me like the cricket in the Sandburg poem, audible even through the deepest dead of winter, so thin a splinter of singing.

൭ౚ

When I first arrive in the area, the entrance of Clinton, South Carolina, is marked by a sign whose style suggests the 1950s: "Welcome to Clinton, City on the Grow." The town has, in fact, been steadily shrinking for years, its movie theater shut down long since, restaurants continuing to disappear overnight, their buildings vacant caverns by the side of the highway. But the sign maintains its staunch tenure on the edge of town.

One side of the railroad tracks houses blacks and Mexicans in crumbling shacks with rusting automobiles parked in dirt driveways. The other side of the railroad tracks, predominantly white, is genteel, pleasant, and quaint, with crepe myrtles lining the roads; azaleas, irises, and roses bursting with color on manicured lawns; and sidewalks gleaming, in excellent repair. It's a Norman Rockwell painting, but deserted and silent much of the time, its citizens off shopping in Greenville or Columbia or holed up in houses to watch TV, blue lights flickering behind curtains.

On weekends, the streets and sidewalks are empty but for the occasional dog walker or panting high school track team, the woman who pushes her small disabled dog in a baby stroller, or the guy who rides his Harley round and round the same block, gunning at stop signs. Clinton is a beautiful town, but it feels oppressive to me, claustrophobic. I rent an apartment ten miles down the road in Laurens, a factory town named for a famous slave trader. Laurens has recently made the national news because of its Redneck Shop, a business that bills itself as the world's only KKK museum and sponsors regular rallies that attract swarms of men in white sheets.

But my townhouse, in a huge wood-and-brick complex, is the most racially and economically integrated neighborhood I find, combining shift workers and teachers, a chiropractor, a contractor, blacks, whites, Mexicans, a Pakistani, families, singles. My place is large and comfortable, but it doesn't feel like a home. The neutral carpet and white walls, the ill-fitted sinks and toilets, and the flimsy, badly designed cabinetry in a kitchen that lacks a silverware drawer—all scream *rental property*. I've always rented, but now I want to settle down. I've thought about buying a house, but where? Maybe I'll adopt the baby first, then figure it out.

I first arrive at my new apartment one rainy August night, my windows so awash I can barely see, after a long day on the road during which I counted 108 U-Hauls, Ryder trucks, and professional moving vans. I duck through a small monsoon to carry a foam mattress, kitchen supplies, and books from my car to the apartment. Then I wait for the movers, to be followed by my parents.

My things arrive, but my parents do not; they cancel their trip because my younger brother is having a crisis, still struggling with the devastation of his wife's desertion. I lie awake for a night consumed by childish resentment that my brother's emotions are more real to my parents than the desolation I feel alone in a new place far from anyone I know. I toss between sleep and waking. I tell myself that I am being silly, that it is only right for all of us to put my niece's needs first.

In the morning I get up and hang my ex-husband's photographs and a painting by my friend Kevin, buy a fish-shaped soap dish for the half bath downstairs, and take my Welcome Wagon coupons to local businesses for free dry cleaning, fitness classes, and candleholders. These are my perfunctory stabs at decorating and becoming a part of my community.

My job begins and time stops. I have little time to think about Sidney, or my parents, or adopting a baby. I'm working all the time, repeatedly startled by my discoveries of how rigidly my new department maintains its policies and traditions. Only in-class writing is allowed, and only in conjunction with objective tests, and only in a four-paragraph, conclusion-free form based on a long-out-of-print textbook the department used decades ago. I'm aghast at how totally these policies violate all of my experience and training, and at the way senior faculty yell at me when I commit what seem to me minor infractions, like leaving the time of the final off my syllabus. I commit a much more major faux pas when in a meeting I question the effectiveness of the department's stiff penalties for students' grammatical mistakes.

This is new to me, supervisors taking me to task like a child, but when I become upset, Caroline, one of the department's joint chairs, assures me that scolding is just part of the culture of the place. I should just yell back and not take it so seriously. The couple of times I follow that advice, my senior colleagues immediately drop ominous comments about my long-term prospects at the institution.

Whenever there is conflict, I step up my efforts to do a good job, working twelve-hour days, eating meals and sleeping so irregularly that I experience precipitous blood sugar drops and often squint through eyestrain so severe my vision blurs and my eyes are puffy. The job market in my field is terrible and I've moved so far from home, I am determined to make things work, but sometimes it feels as if I'm pouring all of my energy into a void. Still I soldier on.

Summer lasts and lasts, refusing to give way to fall. The leaves and grass on my route to school remain startlingly green for weeks. Every day I drive under these eerily green trees canopied over the highway. I pass green kudzu twining around branches and furring telephone poles. Then I hit the strip, zipping by the Wal-Mart where the brands are unfamiliar and the clerks and I don't understand one anothers' accents, and past a sign for Miss Fay, Palm Reader and Adviser, sandwiched between two churches. Then there are yet more green trees, yet more green kudzu, vines rioting across the countryside, wrapping phone wires, strangling all life in its path. Once exalted for its miraculous ability to stop soil erosion through its rapidly growing roots that form a supportive network and enrich the soil, kudzu was planted throughout the South. Now it continues to spread, to multiply, to suffocate everything it encounters, a noxious weed after all.

Sometimes, right before sleep—my only time to plan or daydream or reminisce—I recall how once, back in Nebraska, I woke to the sound of a baby's wail, a loud shriek from the apartment on the other side of the wall.

Then I realized that there was no apartment on the other side, that the cry was from a dream. That I had just heard my own baby, maybe not yet born, maybe on the other side of the world. I needed to go find her. Urgently.

But then I woke all the way, woke to logic and reason. I couldn't go find her. I didn't have a job yet.

Now I have a job, but it consumes all of my energy, all of my emotion. How can I possibly go find my baby?

And I lie and listen to rain swishing on my roof, then slowing to a tick tick, and I feel no more rooted or secure than I did last summer, my last few weeks in Nebraska, when the climate of my home region, my childhood's formative weather, asserted itself with a vengeance. Every day there were wind watches, thunderstorm warnings, tornado sirens. The wind against my upstairs apartment kept me awake at night. It clattered the blinds and battered my nerves. On my ceiling, water formed stains like maps of undiscovered countries, then began to drip. All night I scooted furniture out of the way of each new leak.

When I finally slept, a new leak sprang; rain woke me like cold rage.

I slept again until the roofer and his weird brother started their early morning pounding. The banging set light fixtures swaying and flickering. I gathered hot pads to tighten the bulbs. Rain hammered, hammers rained, and I felt the mounting dry-eyed hysteria of one who never dreams.

Once, rain had made me feel snug and wind had tugged at all my yearnings. Now, instead, when rain scrolls down the windows and nearby screen doors bang rhythmically, I am aware how easily what little I have could blow away.

And then, finally, after a week of rain, the leaves start to change, the kudzu to turn brown. Unlike in the Midwest, where leaves flame red, yellow, and orange overnight, the shift here is more gradual, the trees' outside edges tipped with color that encroaches little by little, the inside leaves still relentlessly green, each tree like a bleached blond whose roots need a touch-up.

By May, I'm numb with exhaustion. Sunny, breezy days stretch before me, with time to read, catch up with old friends, rent videos, do aerobics, cook meals, take naps. Wiped out, I sleep constantly. And more and more, as I'm drifting off or waking, my thoughts turn to the baby I heard crying in a dream.

After the year I've had, adopting a baby would be sheer insanity. Besides, I don't feel a burning desire to become a mom just yet. My arms don't feel empty without a baby, I don't long for the companionship of a child, I don't itch to paint Pooh murals on the spare bedroom walls, I haven't secretly bought a stroller and pushed around sacks of flour or the neighbor's cat. These are the signs I tell myself that I must wait for so I know that I am ready to become a parent. Drowsily, I float away on the drone of a nearby lawn mower while a ghost child pedals by on a trike.

I'm lonely, but it's not the kind of loneliness a child could cure. What I long for are endless late-night conversations with someone I've known for years. What I long for are night swims in a reservoir near Lincoln followed by wee-hour breakfasts at diners with my grad school friends.

As the heat grows more intense, more stifling, I feel more and more rest-

less in this small town where people's social lives revolve around churches. Whenever I work out at the Y or get my hair cut, I overhear endless dis-
cussions of weddings and choir practices and ice cream socials, and I try
not to shudder. I can safely say that this is not a life I want. How can I possibly tie myself down with a child?

But I'll look up from my book and there will be that ghost kid, splash-
ing in a plastic wading pool. Back in Lincoln when I read the book about
single parents by choice, all of those interviewed were much more finan-
cially stable than I am, with emergency accounts containing two years'
wages and savings to cover their future children's college tuition. They belonged to huge, supportive communities and extended families ready to
drop everything and offer casseroles and babysitting. No doubt those single parents also had enough money to take a six-month leave of absence
from work and still afford the salary of live-in help.

Leaving for the grocery store, I find myself calculating the extra time it
would take to buckle a child into a car seat. My head turns inadvertently
when babies strapped in shopping carts pass by. I remind myself of all the
reasons I can't raise a child just yet, but then I'll look over my shoulder and
there will be my ghost child, sticking dried apricots to the car window.

So I think maybe I'll make one or two calls, talk to a couple of agencies.
They'll be kind but firm. They'll tell me to call back in a few years when I
have tenure and savings. They'll suggest that I reexamine my motives,
make sure I'm not just missing my niece or responding to all the social
conditioning that women are supposed to be mothers. They'll tell me I'm
not old enough or young enough or religious enough or maternal
enough—they'll find some reason to turn me down.

It takes me an hour to prepare to make the call. I move the phone to the
spare room, the only room that doesn't share walls with a colleague's
apartment. I unearth a book I bought a while back, listing an agency in
Greenville that handles international adoptions. I close the window so
that my words won't carry out on a breeze to the complex manager kneel-
ing beside the mailboxes, transplanting impatiens and marigolds.

I'm terrified—of what? That asking questions will commit me, that accidentally I will set in motion a process I can't reverse?

I pick up the phone and dial, and all at once my future seems staked to
that one phone call. I am staggered by the power of my longing for a baby,
the feeling that something contained has been unleashed, emerging as if

from a long hibernation. The minute I begin to punch in the numbers, I can never turn back.

Later I will learn that most people who want to adopt internationally do far more research and in many cases choose out-of-state agencies, a perfectly workable arrangement. I mistakenly think I have to use a South Carolina agency, and there is only one listed in my book. It will be a long time before I come out of some weird state of denial to recognize that I've signed on with a fundamentalist Christian organization that focuses on domestic adoption, seeming less interested in their international division. They also prefer to work with married people, particularly conservative ones. Maybe I should have figured some of that out from my first phone call, but by the time the receptionist answers, I am convinced that this agency is my only option.

"I'm thinking about adopting," I tell the receptionist. I'm sitting on the sunbonnet girl quilt patched together by my great-grandmother with scraps from her dresses. Suddenly, it seems unbearable not to pass on this quilt to a daughter.

Normally, I'm the sort of pervert who's amused by those quilts in which each block shows the sunbonnet girl meeting a new gruesome death—attacked by Hale-Bopp, a carjacker, and killer bees, squashed by an elephant, plummeting toward earth clinging to a broken bungee cord. But now here I am, inhabited by this desperately sentimental person who tells the receptionist, "From China. I'm single."

"Oh, I don't think—"

"China will let single people adopt," I say and launch a filibuster about the policies I've read on the U.S. Consulate web page. If I can't win her over with enthusiasm, confidence, and logic, I'll wear her down with my persistence.

Finally, she cuts in, still sounding reluctant. She will have Pat, the social worker, call me back.

Within a few days, I'm filling out a preliminary application just to see if there's any chance I'll be accepted. I earned below poverty level two years ago, when I was still in grad school; I'm sure the agency will frown on this. Pat seems unconcerned. She invites me to the international adoption support group she has organized.

I'm nervous, knowing how unlikely it is that I will fit in. My year in

South Carolina has zapped my social confidence. People smile and say hi but rarely invite me to their gatherings, which are designed for couples with children.

I know that I am too direct and intense for these people, too unwilling to make small talk and observe the niceties of social convention. Probably this is a terrible character flaw, but I don't want to fix it. I don't want to become an indirect smiling person who talks endlessly about pecan recipes and the recent heat spell. I don't see much hope of blending any better into this international adoption support group of fundamentalist Christian couples.

In a narrow room lined by couches and chairs, couples huddle together, holding hands. I sit down quickly, feeling like an intruder. But then I notice a woman sitting in the corner while a blond toddler hangs upside down from her lap. Maybe I'm not the only single person here.

A couple arrives with their new Chinese daughter, getting settled in a bustle of diaper bag, camera case, scrapbooks, and photo albums. Their fourteen-month-old daughter, Caitlin, takes a few steps toward the center of the room, plops onto her diaper, pulls herself up, and plods on.

We all introduce ourselves. Caitlin's parents came back from China four months ago. A couple squished together on half of a couch are also applying to China. "We've had to spend some time grieving that we can't have children, but we're ready," the woman says, her gaze roving between Pat and a couple across the room.

"She's wanted to adopt for a long time, but I was stubborn about seeing the Lord's will," her husband says.

"Then we were at a Chinese restaurant, and my fortune cookie said, 'You will succeed in all that you adopt,'" the wife says.

Her husband looks down into her eyes. "And mine said, 'You are a generous and giving person.'"

We all laugh. I'm a little embarrassed, though; my desire to adopt a child seems like an impulse next to their stable, thought-out decision, even if it was triggered by fortune cookies.

"We should have our baby by Christmas," the wife says. "I'll probably quit my job in November or so. We don't want our child to be raised by day cares."

I shrink a little further into my seat. My child will most certainly attend a day care.

The woman in the corner with the upside-down toddler is, it turns out, a married mom who adopted her little girl from Russia. "I was hoping my husband could come, but he has a late shift," she says. "We've been so busy since we got back. We're working on getting her American citizenship and birth certificate so that when she goes to kindergarten, no one will have to know she's adopted." She looks around, gaze resting on each couple, skimming right past me.

I wait for someone to ask what's wrong with being adopted, or to say something about the importance of being up front about a child's adoption and proud of her heritage, but everyone just nods. It's probably a good sign that they're not being judgmental, I tell myself.

I'm starting to feel both invisible and terribly conspicuous as the others introduce themselves: a couple who want to adopt a sibling group from Guatemala, a couple who already have a biological daughter but want to adopt a son from Korea just as the husband was twenty-five years before.

"I love working, but I've been having to adjust some of my attitudes," the wife says while her Korean American husband nods. "I know I need to be there for my family. Every day I thank the Lord that Ken was willing to accept me as his wife."

Her husband keeps on nodding and doesn't say anything about his luck in having her accept him for her husband.

What am I doing here among all of these married people who take it as a given that it's a woman's role to sacrifice everything for her family? When I introduce myself, I do so quickly. "I want to adopt a baby from China," I say, and everyone averts their eyes without asking me any of the follow-up questions with which they have deluged the others.

I occupy myself with blocking Caitlin from climbing onto the arm of a couch and toppling over the edge. I'm pretty sure I'm blushing, I'm so uncomfortable. All of my doubts gather in a small choir and begin to serenade me, borrowing the voices of disapproving friends who have scolded me in the past for considering raising a child alone; my doubts impersonate relatives who criticize less-than-perfect mothers, including any who don't stay home full-time.

I'm tempted to flee, but then Caitlin's parents start narrating the story of their trip to China. Though they seem to be addressing their comments to everyone but me, I'm too fascinated to stir. "There wasn't a lot of food we could eat," Caitlin's mom says. "I mean, we did find a Kentucky Fried Chicken and we went to McDonald's a few times, and at least there was a Pizza Hut in Guangzhou."

Okay, I tell myself. Obviously I come from a very different world than these people, and maybe they're just ignoring me because they sense my discomfort. Or maybe it's just that no one knows how to define me. Maybe they've never known anyone who chose to become a single parent, or maybe they're wondering where I've stashed my husband. It could be that no one wants to say the wrong thing, make the wrong assumption.

At moments like this, I think back to a formal rush party my friend Ruth talked me into going to back in college, before it became patently clear that I'd rather throw myself in front of a train while guzzling Liquid-Plumr than join a sorority. Lacking a proper dress, I borrowed one of Ruth's mother's garage-sale finds, a long floral Victorian lace-up number with huge drapey witchy sleeves. Everyone else wore simple short white dresses.

"I'm dressed all wrong," I moaned through my teeth to Ruth. "I want to go home."

"Just act like 'but of *course* this is what I'm wearing,' and you'll be fine," Ruth said.

So all evening, as the full skirt bustled around me and my sleeves spilled from my wrists like huge cornucopias capable of holding an abundance of flowers and fruit, I gritted my teeth, thinking fiercely, "But of *course* this is what I'm wearing."

All night, people complimented my marvelous sleeves.

Maybe this sort of confident nonchalance is a skill some people are born with. It's one I have to learn again and again.

And so looking around at the support group, I think that tonight I am setting the tone for my life with my daughter. I have to sound strong, assertive, confident, and matter-of-fact.

No pressure here.

But of *course* I'm going to be a single mother, I think. But of *course* I'm adopting a child.

The words feel unreal to me, as if I'm playacting.

"Were there single parents in your group?" I ask Caitlin's parents.

Everyone looks at me, directly at me for the first time, and it seems that some tension in the room dissolves.

"There were several single ladies," Caitlin's mom says. "They had their mother or a friend along to help out."

"I was planning to go alone," I say.

"Oh, no." Caitlin's mom shakes her head. "It's too strenuous. You'll need moral support and extra hands." She speaks matter-of-factly, as if she fully believes that I am going to go to China to adopt a baby. A little thrill sparks through me. I am going to go to China to adopt a baby!

And I realize that up to that moment I haven't really believed it. I am so excited I can hardly sit still. I watch Caitlin scoot across the floor on her back.

"She must have done that in her crib at the orphanage a lot," her mom tells me quietly. "When we got her, she had a bald spot on the back of her head."

I'm going to adopt a baby! I think, watching Caitlin, barely paying attention to everyone shuddering when Caitlin's dad talks about being asked to participate in a dedication ceremony at a Buddhist temple.

"I've read that China is on its way to becoming a Christian country," one of the husbands says. "Just look at all the countries that live in poverty and war because they've turned their backs on God. I praise the Lord that China is moving in the right direction."

I say softly to his wife, "What are you going to name your daughter?"

"Emmeline," she says. "What about your daughter?"

My daughter. I'm going to have a daughter.

"Sophie," I answer, a little surprised myself to realize that I have decided.

A week ago I spent a sleepless night perusing family trees and finding more ammunition than inspiration—the sorts of names that would one day enable me to say, "Well, I *could* have named you Winifred or Euza or Essic Mac or Modesty Faye." Or "Just be glad you weren't a boy, or you might have ended up an Ebenezer or Leafchild or Elmer Ray or Rufus."

Rufus, after my distant relation William Devane Rufus King. He was sworn in as U.S. vice president in 1853 but died before he could take office.

I once couldn't resist pointing out to my mother the evasive descriptions and sly insults in King's funeral oration, such as

> That immortal triumvirate, Calhoun, Clay, and Webster . . . were just then beginning to exhibit the giant proportions of their unmatched intellects. . . . Among these stood William R. King . . . differing somewhat from them in many of these great attributes of mind.

Through a little research, I discovered that King was rumored to have had a lifelong affair with James Buchanan, whose fiancée committed suicide when she found out. Andrew Jackson considered King so "prissy" he called him "Miss Nancy."

I asked Mom if that's where she got my name. She was not amused. I was named Nancy Grace for two grandmothers, she reminded me, Nancy Jane Geisler and Agatha Grace Whetstone. Dad denies it now, but I remember him telling me that my brother Jeff and I had been named for the comic pages. I was horrified; I felt no kinship, even harbored some disgust, for the cartoon Nancy with the spiky hair. When my little brother Bob was born, I feared that he would be named Mutt, or Beetle, or Sluggo.

That night a week ago I turned through pages of family history, discarding name after name—Myrtle, no, Mahala, no, Sophronia, no. But I'd always been fascinated by those fierce pictures of my great-grandmother Sophronia. It was said that she carried a gun, once fended off an intruder with a red-hot poker, and was nicknamed "Old Sweat" by her husband. I wanted to name my daughter after a strong woman who stood up for herself and admitted to sweating. Some of my other ancestors had nice names: Emma, Isabel, Johannah. I pondered Emma for a while. I liked the literary connections as well as the family ones—Jane Austen's Emma; Emma Lazarus, whose words welcome immigrants. But Sophie just leapt out at me. The name's chief drawback was that my high school sweetheart, with whom I once planned to have children, used to have a cat named Sophie.

When the woman at the support group asks my daughter's name and I say "Sophie," it seems right, inevitable. Sophie from my mom's side, and Grace, from my dad's side, and her Chinese name. Sophie Grace Chinese-name McCabe.

I hope that the right name will ground my child, give her a whole heritage to belong to. Never mind how miserably that strategy failed when my parents tried it on me. I carry the names of my ancestors, I inherited my dad's wavy hair and my mom's blue eyes; I have handwriting spookily similar to my older brother's and a temperament much like my younger brother's. Yet I've always had the feeling that I was born into the wrong family.

After I married and left home for good, I'd return for visits and encounter strange young men, friends of my brothers, lounging around my childhood home, more comfortable there than I'd ever been. Once or twice they demanded to know who I was. They looked skeptical when I identified myself as the daughter or sister. They seemed unaware that there was a daughter or sister.

When I was still living in the Midwest, a friend observed that I had a different accent and speech patterns from the rest of my family—less drawl, crisper inflections, faster rhythms. I had always spoken quickly and clearly, aiming to get a word in edgewise and be heard, not always managing.

I was known as "the dumb one." The one who, as a baby, Dad called a "dizzy blond" because of my pale hair and attempts to crawl forward down stairs rather than backing like normal babies. My parents kept the basement door closed and agreed that it was a wonder I hadn't fallen and suffered brain damage. Or maybe I had, they joked. Maybe that explained things.

How I always put my shoes on the wrong feet, how I never could seem to learn to tell time, how I came out mildly retarded on an IQ test when I was nine. To earn my beads in Campfire Girls, I didn't construct a chemical hygrometer or start my own marimba band. Instead I earned one bead by lowering a glass over a candle, showing that fire could not burn without oxygen. I gained another bead by demonstrating a relaxation exercise, pretending to be a rag doll for five minutes.

Despite all this, I was good at school, my grades consistently higher than those of my brothers. The family myth expanded to accommodate this fact: I wasn't very bright, but I was the one who managed to "follow the rules."

But wait, I protested years later. Wasn't I the child who risked plunging headfirst down the stairs and later resisted learning to tell time? Did those things really show adherence to rules? The baby book my mother kept only sporadically is a record of the things I climbed—when I was ten months old, under "Funny Antics," my mother wrote, "Climbed upon divan using toy on floor as stepping-stone. Climbed upon divan using end table as stepping-stone. Climbed out of crib using brother's bed as stepping-stone."

"Keep your feet off the furniture," Dad kept saying to me when I was a little older, because of my tendency to climb whatever lay in my path, always going over rather than around. Dad threatened that when I grew up, he would come to my house and tromp on *my* couch in muddy shoes. And while he was at it, he would clutter my car floor with candy wrappers and scream in my yard when I tried to work. I laughed hysterically at these images, but I kept climbing over the furniture. When did I ever follow the rules? I asked my parents indignantly, years later.

I should point out that my dad never did wreck my furniture, trash my yard and car, or disturb my work or sleep, but until this last move did the opposite: patiently moved my belongings from apartment to apartment, state to state, assembling desks, hooking up computers, hanging blinds and pictures and toothbrush racks. But in my early twenties, I was so frustrated with the jeering and teasing of my dad and brothers, I resisted going home. I was sick of all the jokes about my inability to properly park a car or distinguish the moon from a streetlight; all I could hear was the hostility behind these jibes, not the affection that my mom claimed was also there.

In the wake of my vehement campaign against the constant taunts, my reluctance to visit, my accumulation of degrees, my divorce and numerous relocations, and some intervention by my mom, the jokes died down. But sometimes I think my entire motivation in life is about escaping those childhood stereotypes: I don't want to follow the rules, at least not the silly ones, and I live in utter terror of being thought dumb, mistaken, foolish, not smart enough.

My parents make their long-postponed visit late in the summer. At lunchtime, they arrive in the car they rented at the airport. They leave their luggage to bring in later and come in to use the bathroom and sit down with glasses of iced tea.

My house smells like Lemon Pledge and the meat I grilled for the fresh chicken salad. There are still vacuum tracks in the carpet, and I've laid out pamphlets from the agency and the videotape they sent me.

Even in the heat, after a day of traveling, my elderly parents look fresh and spry. Dad no longer needs the cane and in retirement has abandoned suits and ties for cool mesh polo shirts. Mom keeps her white hair trim, her glasses on a chain around her neck. Diamond studs glitter in her ears, and she has on a new cotton pantsuit. Mom dumps her huge shapeless purse on the floor, and Dad gulps down his tea and shakes out an ice cube to suck on while I update them. I've attended two support group meetings, and the agency has sent preliminary approval and a fifteen-page formal adoption application that requires numerous supporting documents.

"I thought you might want to watch the video while you're here," I tell them. I'm bothered by the parts where the adoptive parents mention their anti-abortion views, but my parents will approve of them. I just like watching all of the children, all different ages, from all different countries.

"We've been talking about it," Mom says. "We want to come stay with you and take care of the baby when you go back to work. And we'll come babysit when you have to go to conferences."

Dad rattles another ice cube into his mouth.

"We may seem far away, but we can get here in twenty-four hours," Mom goes on. "If she gets the chicken pox or you have an emergency. And you're going to have to come for a month every summer. We want to see her grow up."

For just a second, sitting there cooling my bare knee with the bottom of my tea glass, I believe that this baby is going to gel us into some version of a family we've never been able to achieve. "That's great," is all I can say.

Dad glances at Mom and then leans forward, his characteristic restraint loosening as he says, "We want to go to China with you."

I feel my smile freeze. "Well," I say carefully. "I already asked Jody, actually." I'd e-mailed my cousin weeks ago, asking her if she'd come along. She wrote back a one word reply: "Absolutely!"

"We've always wanted to go to China," Mom says. "You know, when your dad worked for Boeing, he wasn't allowed to visit Communist countries."

"Oh," I say. I smile weakly. Why am I grateful for my parents' offer of help but completely dismayed by this new development?

I turn on the video and go to refill the glasses and make sandwiches, alone with my guilt in the kitchen while my parents murmur in the other room.

The next morning I pack up the car and take them to Columbia on tours of historic houses. The following day, it's the botanical gardens in Clemson. I drive and drive, no longer pumped up when we talk about my baby. Every time the subject comes up, I struggle against panic, feeling greedy, insensitive, horribly selfish for wanting to keep part of my dream for myself.

And so the familiar loop is set in motion: I stay silent out of fear of hurting my parents' feelings. They remain completely unaware of mine. Tension mounts. I begin to interject small protests. "It's so hard for you to keep up," I point out to Mom, who ignores me. "I need to get used to walking long distances if I'm going to go to China," she keeps warbling, even though her knees are giving her so much trouble it takes five minutes to climb the stairs in my apartment. On tours, she lags behind the group. She won't use the public restrooms at a state park because they're too primitive—and we're talking wooden seats and a few flies, not holes in the ground you have to squat over.

"Mom, you can barely walk," I say gently as we head toward a restaurant in the Smokies, right over the North Carolina border.

"Oh, well, I can just stay behind in the hotel and let your dad do the sight-seeing in China," Mom says.

"But Dad, wasn't it in Israel that you hurt your leg?" I ask.

"I shouldn't have climbed all of those steps," Dad says.

"The people in my support group say that the trip is fast-moving and strenuous," I say. "Do you really think it's a good idea?" I know that a typical China adoption trip involves days of paperwork interspersed with massive amounts of touring so that new parents will know something about their children's heritage.

"Well, we can stay back at the hotel if it's too difficult," Dad says.

"But we'll have to rush to catch planes. I'll need help carrying luggage and a baby," I try again.

Dad turns to look out the window. In the back seat, Mom says nothing. I hear her turning the atlas pages. I feel terrible, cruel, but relieved: maybe the silence means that they get it and will drop the subject. A war wages between my guilt and my certainty that it would be a bad idea for them to accompany me.

I have obscure visions of one of my parents hospitalized in China, of something terrible happening. Of, at the very least, trying to lug a baby and all of our suitcases through airports while my parents limp along and planes take off without us.

What it comes down to is, I don't want to go to China to take care of three people. I want to focus on my baby.

My car strains up hills.

"One time, when I was stationed in Okinawa, I accidentally flew into Chinese airspace during a New Year's celebration," Dad says. "I had to get out of there fast. I've always wanted to go back."

He doesn't get it, after all.

I picture my dad as a young man, hovering in the air above the birthplace of his future grandchild, fireworks exploding around the plane.

He seems so old, older all the time. What if this is his last chance to go to China? My heart pumps guilt through my veins. Guilt, guilt, guilt pulses in my wrists, my neck, my temples, I throb with guilt.

By the time we are seated at a table in a log restaurant whose long front porch is lined with rocking chairs, I am coiled so tight it feels like one wrong word, one quick yank, and I am going to fly apart at dizzying speeds.

Mom shuffles off to the bathroom.

"Dad, she can barely walk," I burst out. "I don't think you should be planning to come."

Haven't I been saying things like this all day? Why does Dad look taken aback, as if my protests are news to him? We sit in silence. I wish he would say something. I agonize that I've hurt his feelings, destroyed his dream.

When Mom returns, I fumble to explain. That I want to focus on the baby. That I need them to be well-rested in the United States to help me. That I will worry about them if they're with me.

"Why should you worry?" Mom asks, genuinely puzzled.

A web of fine lines has deepened a bit more in Mom's skin each time I see her; Dad's chin has a tremor. The veins on the backs of their hands are closer to the surface, ropier; age spots freckle the skin. When I acknowledge that my parents are aging, that their deaths are inevitable, I feel as if I'm somehow speeding my parents toward them. Best not to say anything, to stick with the kindness of denial rather than the brutality of truth, the mean and heartless acknowledgment of a heartbreaking reality.

Mom shrugs. "We just want to do what you want," she says.

But Dad stays silent. There is no clue on his impassive face. Is he hurt and reproachful, or simply taking things in stride?

My dad has never said much. When I was a child, he resented being the breadwinner we all took for granted. I had no idea how much our distance and childish sense of entitlement made him feel that he wasn't real to us. I had no idea until I was an adult and my mother told me.

We pay at the register, then cross the bridge to the gravel parking lot.

"When you adopt, you're a lot less prepared than if you've been pregnant for nine months," Dad says out of the blue. "When someone just hands you a baby, it's much harder to adjust."

I unlock the car door. "No one just hands you a baby," I snap. "Nobody who's pregnant has to go through extensive background checks and get letters of recommendation and medical tests before they're allowed to have the baby."

"I just think it's harder to adjust to the limits on your freedom," Dad says.

Does he really think I have some freewheeling lifestyle I'm too selfish to give up? Sometimes I think that while he's proud of my education and career, he disapproves of the ways I don't live up to his image of how women should be, nurturing, self-sacrificing, peacekeeping at all costs.

"You think women who are pregnant are automatically better parents?" I ask.

"No, just more prepared," Dad answers calmly from the back seat.

My sister-in-law gave birth at the age of twenty, and I know that she loves my niece, but she couldn't have been less prepared to be a mother. Where are my dad's comments coming from? Is he trying to get back at me for not wanting him to come to China, implying that I'll be a less-than-adequate mother?

Mom jumps in, arguing with my dad, citing everyone she's ever known who adopted and reviewing all the things they did to prepare.

Dad won't budge.

"Well, I think you're smart to skip morning sickness and labor pains," Mom says.

By now, I'm crazed with frustration. I'm not adopting a baby as a substitute for giving birth. My dad's seeming disapproval nags at me. Should I have just agreed to let them come to China with me? But no. If I'm going to be a parent, I have to stop caring whether my family approves of me. I have to be able to speak out on behalf of myself and my child; I have to make decisions that allow me to best take care of her.

Still, my anxiety is rapidly turning to terror. In huge ways, no matter how much support I have, I'm going to be doing this all alone.

The conversation dies away. My car struggles up hills and then coasts down. The argument continues in my head, all the ways I wish I'd responded tangling with all of my insecurities and fears: maybe I just can't do it alone; maybe I just don't have the right personality to be a good parent.

Staring out the back window, Dad might be thinking about his garden or the books he wants to read, not about how I've disappointed him. He's one of those silent people onto whom others always project wisdom and judgment. Maybe he isn't thinking about my potential as a parent at all.

The next morning he goes to Wal-Mart and buys plants for my patio. After a night's sleep, I decide that he was just musing aloud and put his foot in his mouth, then, cornered, he kept trying to defend himself until offhand comments took on the dimensions of a moral position. And yet I still feel sick, worried. How can I, such an oddball, so unmaternal, so unprepared, so unsure about my long-term future in my job, fill out this paperwork? I abandon the pile on my desk. I don't have the heart to think about it right now.

My neighbors compliment the plants hanging from my patio fence and lining the concrete. "The potted plants stage," they say sagely. They are also transplanted midwesterners. The patio additions are apparently a predictable part of the family visit cycle when, with too little to do and after too much togetherness, having exhausted all of the tourist sites and restaurants, your only options in this isolated place are watching tensions escalate and going shopping at the Wal-Mart garden center.

But the thought continues to nag at me: maybe in some ways my dad knows me better than I know myself. Deep down I suspect that I'm not constitutionally suited to parenthood, I, who could never keep a plant much less a pet alive. Sometimes I wonder if my childhood of lost pets didn't leave with me a form of attachment disorder. Or maybe I was just born without maternal instincts.

One weekend when I was little, Dad built a chicken-wire structure in the back yard. Black and white *American Pigeon Journals* began appearing in our mailbox. Dad paged through them in the evenings, burping in a quiet, authoritative way. It was much later that I learned that burping was not an expression of intellectual superiority, a symbol of erudition along the lines of professorial pipe smoking or leather elbow patches. It was much later that I realized that my dad's burping was a result of lifelong digestive problems and might have been embarrassing to him.

Eventually, Dad took me along to pick out some pigeons. The birds looked faded and musty, not beautiful as I'd imagined, not the purest snow white or exotic rainbow colors I expected of pet birds. As they trilled on wooden perches and propelled themselves into the air above, I cringed. They reminded me of darting rodents with tiny twitching heads. I was horrified by the violence with which they battered each other in frenzies of wings.

"Why don't you pick one out?" Dad said.

I pointed at the ugliest one, gray-brown like lint, because I just wanted to escape that barn.

From then on, the sound of trilling and the beating of wings was a constant, accompanying walks down the driveway from the school bus, summer afternoons picking strawberries from the garden, Saturdays reading next to an open window. The floor of the chicken-wire cage turned to hard-packed dirt, a bald spot in the yard.

Mom never went near the pigeons. "Ugh," she said.

I secretly agreed, but my revulsion made me feel guilty. I tried to make it up to Dad by acting interested in the birds. Many mornings I went with him to feed them. As he filled the trays with a corn and sunflower seed mixture, he warned me never to touch the eggs.

"Ugh," I wanted to say, but instead I nodded, watching the sharp beaks. The babies were even uglier, naked and blind. I couldn't imagine wanting to touch them.

When I begged for a real pet, a cat or a dog, Dad said he was afraid it might bother the pigeons.

I appealed to Mom, but all she said was "Ugh." She was, it turned out, as disgusted by furry creatures as by feathered ones.

"Why don't you like animals?" I asked her.

"I guess I just had a warped childhood," Mom said.

I never could figure out what she meant. I tried to picture a childhood swollen like a door that would no longer fit its frame or wavy like the air above a barbecue grill. I worried that my revulsion for Dad's birds might be the result of something warped I didn't know how to recognize in my own character, my own childhood.

People were always dumping cats out near the city limits sign a block from our house. Stray cats stalked the pigeon cage, pawing through the wire and yowling while birds rose in clashes of wings to take refuge in the shed, from which they peered with dumb bobbing heads.

"Scat!" Dad yelled at the cats.

I put out bowls of dry food on the back porch and sat there for hours, waiting to win their trust. Mom brought sacks of dry cat food from the store, but she refused to let any animal set foot in the house.

Eventually, every cat I adopted died on one of the highways that bordered the house. I got so used to it, my tender heart toughened. I ceased to cry at each new death and learned to check the road for my pets every day when I dismounted the bus steps. Scanning the road soon became a family habit. Mom felt bad about refusing to allow the cats to live in the house, away from the danger, but she did not give in. When she was a child, it had been inconceivable to feed stray animals when there were hungry people or to take sick animals to a vet when there were children who lacked medical care. So her regular grudging purchase of cat food was, I knew, the most I could expect.

"I just don't want the filthy things in the house," I heard her tell someone on the phone, sighing. And then that mysterious phrase again: "I guess I just had a warped childhood."

When I was eleven or twelve, a pregnant stray cat turned up on our side porch. So many of my pets had died on the highways surrounding our house, I didn't want another. But what could I do when I saw the fur stretched tight over bones, when I heard the hollow hunger in the animal's yowls before she skittered off through the chin-high grass in the vacant lot two houses down? I fed her, and when she warmed to me, she let me lay my hand against the quick pulsations of her bulging sides.

I heard the sound, like baby birds, before I parted the bushes. The cat, a dark shape with glowing yellow eyes, squatted under a tangle of twigs and leaves. She backed away from me, plopping onto the squirming shapes, but not before I saw that there were four of them, a keyboard of kittens: white, black, white, black.

Gently, I reached under the cat, drawing out a black kitten and staring into its closed little face, its pink mouth that sucked at air. The whiskers, nostrils, hooked claws, thin slices of eyes: they were impossibly tiny and perfect. Under the fur, those frail skeletons could so easily give way in my hands. I was terrified at my surge of tenderness, my ferocious desire to squeeze those tiny creatures, my knowledge that they were too fragile to bear the power of my overwhelming love. The cat followed me nervously till I returned the kittens to her, and then her pink tongue lapped away my scent.

Again and again I was drawn back to stare at those kittens, to cup them in my hands, to touch velvet nose-tips and sandpaper tongues. And then, late that day, when I pulled apart the bushes, I couldn't quite register the sight before me. Beside the placid cat lay a kitten's disembodied head.

My scream rode high above the chirping birds and passing cars, brought my dad running.

"You handled them too much," he explained gently. "It made their mother nervous. She thought she was protecting them."

For years I believed this, and maybe it was true, even though a friend said, long afterward, "It wasn't your fault. Cats are like people—some of them are just bad parents." So when I wonder what kind of parent I will be, when I wonder what my dad can see that I can't, I remember how even when my hands resisted the fleeting impulse to crush a kitten's tender bones, even when I thought I had averted danger, my merest touch could, after all, do irreparable harm.

Something in me went numb with the loss of all of those pets. Once, as an adult, I took in a hamster—a mistake, I quickly realized. It was like I no longer had the capacity to care about small furry creatures. Sigmund was an elderly little animal, retired patriarch of the hamster lab at the school where I taught. I bought him a cage and some plastic tunnels and a little wheel.

Sigmund spent every waking hour trying to escape. He banged his head against the cage's metal lid, he poked his nose against the air holes and butted his head against them, he squished his face against the cage's plastic sides. I felt cruel and out of sorts, living with such blatant dissatisfaction. And when, one day, he escaped, and bared his teeth at me, hissed, and darted behind the fridge, the lines were drawn: I was his captor and he was vermin. I dutifully cleaned his cage and gave him food and water, but there was no affection in our enslavement to each other.

What if I'm no more cut out to be a mom? What if I adopt a baby and want to give it back?

But despite all my doubts, the good student in me kicks up, the one who can't bear to be seen as flighty, the one who hates to abandon a book halfway through or leave a project unfinished. As soon as my parents leave, I take up the paperwork again. I'll just finish filling it out, see what happens.

After all, I remind myself, I can back out at any time.

2

First day of Chinese class: Ping Ping starts with initials. She sings a sound at us; we sing back our attempts at imitation.

"B," she sings, and we reply, "B."

"P," she sings, and we sing it back.

And so on, through *g* and *k, h, l, n,* and then the finals: *a, o, i, u, ao, an, ie.* We are a choir of Chinese consonants and vowels. She pronounces *ie* twice; it sounds like "Yah."

"Ie Ie," she sings.

"Ie Ie," we answer.

"Ie Ie," she tries again.

"Ie Ie." We don't miss a beat.

"Ie," she says.

"Ie," we sing back, Chinese bebop.

"This is funny?" she asks a sophomore.

Smiles vanish. "Ie Ie," we go on singing.

Ping Ping focuses on us one at a time, waits for each solo echo. When she sings at me and I sing back, she pauses doubtfully, stares at me a second, and says, finally, "Well, okay."

Already I am failing to speak my child's language. Most people have till adolescence before the language barrier really kicks in.

Next are the four tones. First tone is high-pitched.

"Bā," Ping Ping sings out.

"Bā," we repeat, a choir again, her obedient echo.

Second tone: "Bá," Ping Ping says, a question, her voice straining onto tiptoes.

"Bá," we repeat.

Third tone: "Bǎ," she says, a sound that falls into a hole but then crawls out.

"Bǎ," we repeat. I try not to dip my head.

Fourth tone: "Bà," she finishes, a definitive little jump, an exclamation point.

Next is sound and tone discrimination.

Ping Ping sings, we repeat, it's a lightning round of sounds:

"Bō bò."

"Bō bò."

"Pā pà."

"Pā pà."

"Pī pì . . ."

Swiftly, we all form these sounds, our imperfect syllables, we sing each long note and then each staccato one, faster and faster, chorusing, then soloing on command, until I half expect us to burst into *Doe a deer a female deer, ray a drop of golden sun* and find ourselves whirling in the Alps wearing clothes made of old drapes.

During the first week, Ping Ping reviews types of strokes: rising, falling, dot, hook. She shows us stroke order: horizontal before vertical, top to bottom, left to right, outside to inside. I try to write my name but can't master the art of keeping strokes in proportion to each other. That's the point at which my work and my adoption paperwork get the best of me, and I give up on characters.

But when Ping Ping speaks, when I study, I picture the tones, the syllables, the strokes. When I reach each new milestone in the paperwork process, I am giddy. My life is a fast and high rising stroke zipping to the top of the page, a vapor trail looping behind a trick airplane, it is leaping and dancing all over the place, across the Alps, wearing old drapes.

Although I ignore the characters, I zealously throw myself into learning how to say, "I am not a doctor," "I am your mother," and "Here is the pictorial I borrowed."

"I am not a doctor" sticks because "bu shi," the equivalent of "am not," sounds, on the tape, like "bullshit." The guy on the tape, Gubo, seems quite vehemently offended that anyone should mistake him for a doctor, pronouncing the words with clipped precision: "Wa bu shi daifu."

I nudge one of my classmates, who also happens to be one of my own students. "Does *bu shi* sound like *bullshit* to you?" I ask.

She looks a little shocked, then listens thoughtfully to a replay of the dialogue. Her face transforms. I doubt that she'll ever forget how to deny that she's a doctor, either.

Outside of class, I corner my fellow students and quiz them about the health and professions of their mothers, their fathers, their older brothers and younger sisters, their friends, their father's older sisters and their mother's younger brothers.

Due to vocabulary limitations, the only answers that my classmates can offer and that I can understand are "He/she is fine. He/she is not a doctor." Still, we speak regularly and continuously enough that bystanders look impressed. We decide to show off a little and start discussing the ownership of various books and pens.

One day I am bragging about my newly acquired skills when a colleague interjects, "But no one in China has brothers or sisters anymore."

While this is not entirely true—the generations before the one-child policy do have siblings, as do many children whose parents are able to pay fines or who live in areas where enforcement is less diligent—my fervor takes a dive. When am I ever going to have the chance to return a pictorial I've borrowed from someone Chinese?

And then one day, I turn the page of the Chinese text and there is no more pinyin, only characters. I am up bu shi creek, so to speak.

At first, adoption paperwork consumes most of my spare seconds— forms for the agency, for U.S. Immigration, and for the Chinese government. In between teaching, preparing classes, marking papers, hosting visiting writers, and attending meetings, I am busy requesting references, ordering copies of birth and marriage certificates and my divorce decree, developing pictures of my townhouse, photocopying years of income tax telefile worksheets, asking the dean for a verification of employment, dropping by the police station for a criminal clearance, applying for a passport, and lining up extra jobs. Between teaching additional classes and workshops, doing freelance writing and editing work, and applying for a federal tax credit and assistance from the South Carolina Department of Social Services, I can just about pay the entire cost of the adoption. I'm not sure how I'll support the baby once I have her, but I'll figure it out when I get there.

When I return to the police station to be fingerprinted for INS, a poker-faced officer asks me, "Why don't you just get married and have babies like everyone else?" And then, in an ominous drawl approaching a growl, he adds, "Or don't you like men?"

I don't think much about this. Women who are single and not always lamenting it get used to being accused of hating men.

First the officer cracks my knuckles—to limber my hands, he says. He turns and twists my fingers into the ink pad and presses hard onto the card.

As he handles my hands roughly, he looks secretly amused, as if I am a crime suspect on whom he is taking subtle revenge. Or maybe I just imagine that his fingers seek out my cuts and scrapes and that his sneer is directed toward my unladylike hands.

I feel defensive on their behalf, these hands with strong muscles and prominent veins and a great big writing callous, not to mention, on most days, lots of paper cuts and ink stains.

The officer keeps barking out criticism: my unpolished nails are all bitten off, my fingers secrete too much oil. I feel like I am being accused of not bathing. I feel smelly and unfeminine, secreting oil.

Sweat blurs my loops, whorls, and arches, the truest measure of identity, the whole time that his gaze turns me into someone I'm not. As he rotates my hands as if they are inanimate objects, I think about how I cut my nails constantly so I can type fast and play the keyboard. I think about my efforts to relearn pieces from my childhood, playing "Nobody Knows the Trouble I've Seen" cross-handed about a thousand times last winter when I was feeling especially lonely and homesick. I think about all the times these hands have followed a spine into the valley of a lover's back, loosening every muscle. I think about the way the tip of my index finger used to fit perfectly into the scar on another lover's cheek. This guy sees dry skin and ringless fingers; I see fingers that have mesmerized a small child with their itsy-bitsy spiders and little bunnies fufu, and palms that have sent her swing flying into a blurred afternoon sun.

Finally the man releases my hands and sends me to wash them. As I leave, he calls out, "Bring us a boy. We have enough girls."

"Oh, it'll be a girl," I say, and escape.

Later I tell my fingerprinting story to Pat and the international adoption support group: They are sympathetic and indignant, even a little angry at the question, "Why don't you just get married and have babies like everyone else? Or don't you like men?"

I assume that they are indignant because of his rudeness, and because even married people sometimes can't have babies "like everyone else." I am pleased that they are put out at the idea that my choice to adopt a child has anything to do with my feelings about men. I am pleased that the conservative Christians in my support group are willing to see me as a full person who doesn't deserve to be insulted by the police officer.

Then, driving home, it hits me. Everyone was so upset on my behalf because the guy was implying that I was a lesbian. I've always been sort of slow. Once a drunk lesbian who misunderstood my friendliness said, as we sat crowded close together at a full table in a bar, "I had no idea. You seemed so straight," and I responded, completely clueless, "Well, I am. I mean, I'm drinking a Diet Coke."

I am accustomed to dumb stereotypes, so I just shrug off the fingerprinting incident. For years, people have assumed I'm selfish, emotionally shallow, or living in luxurious freedom simply because I'm single. Since I decided to adopt, I've generally been getting the selfless saint treatment, which makes me even more uncomfortable than being considered vacuous and flighty. So now I am a lesbian who, unlike any lesbian I know, categorically hates men.

I am less concerned by this than by the fact that my agency's outdated information leads to the rejection of my fingerprints by the INS, whose regulations have changed so that they now only accept fingerprints from agencies that strictly follow certain procedures. I don't question this much; I have entered the mindset of those who adopt internationally and gradually give up trying to figure out the capriciousness of bureaucracies. I follow directions and drive to a Designated Fingerprinting Agency in Greenwood, where a guy completes the task without cracking my knuckles, twisting my wrists out of joint, or speculating on my feelings about men. He seals my fingerprints in an envelope and sends me to wash my hands.

Other than the lack of harassment, the chief difference between the Laurens Police and the Designated Fingerprinting Agency is the quality of the soap, lemony grainy stuff that removes all the ink.

Pat comes to my house for the last home study visit. I wait for her to inspect for poisons under my sinks and run lead tests on my walls, but she doesn't want to be intrusive, so she only gives the house a cursory glance. I practically have to drag her upstairs to show her where the baby will sleep. Apparently the agency doesn't care whether you've organized your closets or bleached your toilet bowls; they just have to make sure there's no visible child pornography or freebasing equipment.

My home study is completed and sent to the Department of Social Services. I send off my paperwork to Immigration. I finish assembling documents for my China dossier, get them all notarized and state certified, and then wait for approval from DSS and INS, all the while feeling like someone impersonating someone who is adopting a child.

I go to the adoption support group regularly. I must want this baby, because although I have trouble not speaking out in my job when I'm troubled by attitudes or policies, here I'm managing to shut up. I smile blankly and change the subject when group members ask if I've found a church yet or advise me to marry a Promise Keeper. When couples in the group experience setbacks and delays, one mom-to-be, Lynn, says, with a wise twinkle in her eye, "God is still preparing you to be parents. He must not think you're quite ready yet." During a major delay of their own, Lynn and Matt arrive at a meeting looking drawn, sagging against each other, Lynn's interpretation of this setback slightly different: "The devil is trying to keep babies from good Christian homes," she says.

I recoil at this, but I keep going to the support group. For different reasons and in different ways, we're all waiting for the same thing, and for the first time in my life, I feel a connection that sometimes transcends all of our differences. Lynn keeps bringing me bags of clothes, baby Birkenstocks and high-top tennis shoes and tiny cotton socks and a little hooded sweatshirt. My baby might never be the right size for these things, but Lynn knows how important it is to let the feet of a ghost baby claim territory in my house, to line a shelf with the Birkenstocks and high-tops, the shiny plastic church shoes with ribbons and bows and the sturdy little walking shoes, to enter a room and find them disheveled as if in the middle of a dance.

ॐ

My last summer before I am due to become a parent, in between working extra jobs for the Educational Testing Service and a summer arts program for high school kids, I nest. I move furniture, combining my bedroom and office to make room for the baby, hauling books to my office on campus, installing a new phone line for my modem, refinishing my kitchen table, having the bathtub resurfaced, calling the cable company out to remove huge coils of cable that look like nests for an ostrich family. I buy a rocker, and I launder and hang hand-me-down baby clothes. Mom and Dad are coming in August with Sidney's old crib. They are going to help me fix up my makeshift changing table and assemble a wardrobe.

At first after they arrive, things hum along. I empty the nooks and crannies of Sid's old car seat, packed full of the crumbled leaves she industriously tore up throughout every car ride. Then I scrape grime from the straps with an old toothbrush while Dad unloads the crib, washing the headpiece and the footpiece and laying the mattress in the sun to dry out its accumulation of moisture during the rainy trip.

Mom takes charge of converting the industrial-looking table that used to serve as a desk into a changing table and all-purpose surface. I've drawn a design for a cover, with a door and windows cut into the part that drapes to the floor, turning the space underneath the table into a playhouse. I have no actual skills to carry out my plan, but Mom brings her sewing kit and machine.

By the second day we are getting along well, clicking even, me describing what I picture, her getting it, then going one better. While Dad patiently sorts all the boards and screws and hinges for the wardrobe, Mom sets to work cutting out big felt tulips for the front of the house and smaller ones for a potted plant to go in the window. I travel upstairs and down, consulting, holding boards steady, fixing lunch, watching my house transform.

Dad brings in the crib mattress and bedslats, the headpiece and footpiece.

"I'll just stack these somewhere and put the crib together next time I come," he says. "I forgot to bring the hardware."

I stare after him. Next time he comes? When will that be? If all goes according to schedule, I'm supposed to have a baby in four or five months.

"But—" I say. "But I wanted the crib to be ready."

I've pictured sitting in my rocker all fall, next to a crib complete with sheets, stuffed animals, and bumper pads, thinking about my baby. I've imagined arriving home from China and laying my baby in her crib and watching her sleep, here in our peaceful house, just her and me. I don't want to navigate my way around a heap of boards for months. I don't want to bring my baby home and then have to wait for my dad to come along and put together the crib.

"I would have to jury-rig it and I'd rather not do that," Dad says cheerfully.

"But you won't be back until after the baby's here," I say. "Where will she sleep?"

"We'll be back to help take care of the baby," Dad answers. "There's plenty of time."

"But—" I say again. "But I really want it all put together." I don't want to be that dependent on him. I want time alone with my baby. I want help, but I also want to be capable of taking care of her alone.

"It will be put together." Dad shrugs.

"No, I mean this week." I am trying to be gentle and polite, but as in my job, the more courteous I am, the more I feel dismissed. In my family and, I'm finding, in at least this pocket of the South, women are expected to be diplomatic by expressing no opinions or desires.

"I'd rather find the original hardware than jury-rig it," Dad explains again, patiently, as if I am brain-damaged.

"But what if something happens before you can get back?" I stop short of pointing out that his health has been shaky the last few years. "I just want one less thing to worry about," I say. My effort to be mild but assertive and firm is getting me nowhere.

Dad just sighs. He clearly has no intention of assembling the crib. I walk away, speechless with helplessness, frustration, and anger. I go upstairs, trying to figure out why I am angry over such a little thing. Or is it such a little thing?

Maybe that's why I'm angry: because I always end up feeling like what I want is insignificant. Because Dad makes me feel like a demanding, ungrateful daughter. Because he never really understands me or pays attention to what I need. Because he's not going to be here forever, and he's acting like he is.

I sit down abruptly on my bed, fear pulling me down like gravity. Because he isn't going to be here forever.

I close the door, hiding out in my room like a moody adolescent, feeling unreasonably irritated with my kind parents, my old, slow, well-meaning parents who just don't get it.

They've driven two days from Missouri to bring me this stuff and help me. Already, they've accomplished far more than I could have alone. Why, after three days, do I feel like an anal-retentive neurotic with ridiculously high expectations? I pace, feeling cramped, cooped up, drained, and downright mean.

Only four days ago I was a virtuous, considerate daughter who picked out two kinds of sugarless cereal for my diabetic mother, and, for my dad, the kind of cookies he likes minus the nuts he's allergic to. I bought them 2 percent milk because they think my skim tastes like water. I bought new sheets for the guest bed. And what about all those letters I've written them in the past telling them how pleased I am by their enthusiasm, how much I want them to be a part of my child's life?

Am I being so unreasonable? I remember the times my dad has had to wait in the car while Mom and I went into a store because all of a sudden his stomach started bothering him. I remember the times he's had trouble walking and the time he ended up in the hospital when he had a temporary short-term memory loss while helping me move. Is it so awful of me to recognize his limitations, to need to be an adult who isn't dependent on him? But would I be feeling so frustrated if I weren't already so dependent on him? After all, I'll never figure out how to get the crib put together by myself.

I agonize, fret, and rationalize, and then I decide that this time, I get to be unreasonable. I'm going to have to stop being my parents' child and become my child's advocate, no matter how unreasonable that will make me.

So I resolutely return downstairs. I feel like the single most inflexible daughter on the planet telling my parents that I really, really need the crib to be ready, that I can't wait.

My parents get those startled, puzzled looks that are their response to anything I feel strongly about. Dad shrugs and goes off to the hardware store.

The crib seems pretty sturdy once Dad gets it assembled, but I dislocate my thumb whenever I try to raise or lower the side.

That's just what you deserve, says the guilty little voice in my head.

All fall, I rock in that room next to the crib. Across from me, black felt letters spell out "Sophie's House," colorful tulips sprout across cloth, and a dog peers out from one curtained window. I rock, my house in order.

∂ℰ∂

I always vaguely expected that during the months before I became a parent, I would feel ephemeral, able to rise and float above the petty world. I imagined feeling more in tune with nature, leaves and rocks and snowflakes gaining the kind of sudden details and sharp clear edges that new glasses give them. I would immerse myself in music and books and daydreams about my baby, calmly moving toward parenthood in my own little sphere of joy and anticipation.

Instead my life remains bogged down in bewildering, petty politics and exasperation with policies, procedures, and perceptions that make little sense to me. I discover that a senior colleague, a hearing-impaired guy named Benjy, has been telling my students not to mind my tactlessness because I am not, after all, a southerner.

I'm sure that I've said my share of thoughtless things in my life, so maybe it's karmic that suddenly I have a reputation for tactlessness based on the fact that Benjy apparently mishears and misquotes a great deal of what I say. Soon I receive a vague administrative reprimand for not being more diplomatic, but I cannot get any of my supervisors to explain what prompted it. The mysterious letter suggests that I should always "think and think again" before I speak.

"Do you think maybe you could remind Benjy that he's deaf?" I ask Caroline, unable to believe that I am being condemned because a hearing-impaired man can't hear me.

Be less direct, Caroline advises me and my fellow junior faculty member, Caddy, a northeasterner. Be southern ladies. Get what you want through smiles, soft voices, subterfuge. Let men think the ideas are theirs.

Caddy and I hoot. Despite her high-heeled pumps, she has the firm, building-vibrating tread of a truck driver; her booming voice echoes in the halls. I am equally, if more subtly, hopeless: no matter how high the hairdresser poufs my hair, no matter how many times I verbally bless people's hearts, I am never going to pull off the southern lady thing. Caddy and I laugh raucously at the very futility of Caroline's suggestions and go on doing things the wrong way, me even more than Caddy. She just slips up occasionally while I feel constitutionally unable to follow protocol.

As I wait for my baby, I find myself stumbling yet again. One day in the dining hall, Benjy blows up at me because I want to become a contributing editor for a grammar handbook. The department has already approved three different workbooks for use in the remedial class, so I didn't anticipate the angry response when I propose temporarily incorporating another choice.

"We all have to do the same thing in our classes or students will talk!" Benjy yelps before scooping up his tray and slamming off, prompting a guy from biology to say, "Wow, do they always order you around like that?"

When I go to talk to Caroline, Benjy has already informed her that I yelled at him and made a scene at lunch. I had indeed talked loudly—Benjy encourages us to do so because with all the dining hall noise, he can't hear otherwise. Caroline sympathizes with my side of the story, but she also warns me that I must not talk to anyone outside the department about our conflicts.

I gape at her, seized by a creepy feeling of déjà vu. I recall all of those books about children of alcoholics that my friends passed around in the late eighties. The key ingredient that supposedly kept family members locked in the shame and silence that embedded them in codependent systems was family loyalty: explicit or implicit injunctions not to betray the secret of the illness around which the family revolved. I used to scoff at these books and at the way friends in therapy overzealously diagnosed the rest of us. But now here I am, right in the middle of my own textbook case of a dysfunctional family system.

Even our department is structured like a family, with joint chairs, a man and a woman near retirement age; sometimes we even jokingly refer to them as "Mom and Dad." We have several big brothers, and then there's Caddy and me, vying for attention and approval.

Caroline is very good to me. Whenever I need to vent, she clears off her rocking chair and feeds me chocolate from her secret stash. So I feel really bad that the minute I leave her office, I seek out friends outside the department for a reality check. I also begin following up all of my conversations with Benjy with e-mail summaries, to which he almost always responds, "Oh! I misunderstood"—though he never forgives me for embarrassing him at the dining hall.

I don't feel much confidence about becoming a parent when my professional life often feels so oddly askew. I work like mad to infuse life into any class that seems sluggish, to shift gears when one approach doesn't work, to be alert for confused or bored students. I'm killing myself to be diplomatic with my colleagues, to follow through on commitments, to attend meetings and finish projects, and I'll sail along happily for a while garnering lots of approval and praise, feeling better about my job, only to turn another corner and confront another bout of mysterious displeasure from my senior colleagues, typically based on rumors and misperceptions I don't know how to change.

By October, feeling stagnant in a job that provides few challenges I can address head-on and oblique criticisms I'm not sure how to tackle, my adoption plans stall as well. There's a rumor on the China adoption list-serv that the group of dossiers that includes mine is on its way to the matching room. I could be assigned a baby any day.

But when the phone finally rings, it brings other news. First, my doctor calls—says something about possible cancerous cells. Medical terminology and explanations of procedures fly by as if I am going a hundred miles per hour past mile markers on a highway.

On the Internet, people from my group start joyfully reporting referrals. "REFERRAL!!!" their subject lines say, or "BABY!!!" or "IT'S A GIRL!" I push the delete button every time I see someone else's good news. I didn't used to be like this. I'm too tense to be generous anymore.

And then, the phone again: Pat.

"This is not your referral," Pat says.

My referral has, in fact, been delayed. The Center for China Adoption is concerned that I might not be heterosexual.

I've seen something about this on the listserv, that the Chinese government has clued in to the fact that for years gay and lesbian couples have been adopting babies. The government recently instituted an explicit rule that all adoptive parents must be heterosexual.

According to the national agency, Pat says, all single applicants are being asked to write statements swearing that we do not have same-sex roommates.

I sit in front of the computer for an hour. "I do not have a same-sex roommate," I type. And then I add, "I do not have any roommates at all."

Will this be enough for them? Will my referral continue to be delayed if the Chinese government isn't convinced?

I type and delete and type and delete and finally let stand, "I am heterosexual."

Writing that sentence feels like a betrayal of everything I believe. That my sexuality is no one's business. That labels are always lies because sexuality exists on a spectrum. That, even though I am in fact heterosexual, I am selling out.

I go to bed in a crisis of conscience and wake up with a plan. I will write a statement attesting that I am a five-toed sloth and send that along with the heterosexuality statement to be notarized and state certified.

Someday I'll show the five-toed sloth statement to my daughter.

"I would have said almost anything to get you," I will tell her.

I take a listserv poll and find only one other prospective single parent who has been flagged by China as "potentially gay." Jennifer in Salt Lake City had to write an affidavit swearing that she will marry should an appropriate man become available.

Soon after I mail my affidavit, the doctor calls with the results of my biopsy. Although I am fine, after all, and although the doctor starts out by saying that no one knows what causes cervical cancer and that there is no evidence that I am in particular danger of it, she nevertheless delicately advises curbing my probably promiscuous activity. I do live in a county with one of the highest incidence per capita of STDs, according to some of my students, so it's a speech she probably has to make. But it seems like a huge cosmic irony, me getting a lecture about my supposed heterosexual habits at the same time that China is delaying my match due to my potential homosexuality.

Lynn from the international adoption support group calls to reassure me. She has discovered through her direct pipeline to God that my referral is being delayed not because I'm still being prepared to be a parent or because the devil is keeping babies from good Christian homes; my referral is simply taking a long time because God is testing my commitment, since as a single person I presumably haven't demonstrated much of it before.

By March I'm crazed from waiting, highly irritable, and prone to lapsing into despair. And then Pat calls with the name of my child.

It turns out to be wrong, a miscommunication from the home office— Ni Qiano Qian, sounding more Hispanic than Chinese. At least I have taken enough Chinese to suspect that something is off.

I call Sara. Definitely not a Chinese name, Sara says. I am expecting my baby's name to mean something like "Beautiful Flower" or "Lovely Blossom." But the closest translation Sara can find for Ni Qiano Qian is "small fleck of rice in the front hall."

Pat tells me that she will receive the FedEx package with my baby's picture in two days. I make an appointment to meet Pat at her office.

For months I've been walking down streets watching little kids, thinking, Could I love that baby? That one? Usually I've thought that I probably could. Then a couple from my adoption support group passed around pictures from their China trip, and I couldn't stop staring at this one poor baby with a Neanderthal forehead and an angry rash.

Oh, no, I thought, maybe not that one.

So while I wait to see my baby's picture, I fret that she will be so peculiar-looking that I will never be able to bond with her. I scold myself for entertaining such a stupid fear, since I have often considered myself peculiar-looking and ought to feel more natural affinity for a small fleck of rice in the front hall than a lovely blossom.

When Pat passes me the paperwork, it turns out that my baby's name is Ni Qiao Qin. Ni is a surname given to all the babies at that orphanage; it means "a person or small child." Qiao Qin means *smart and musical*. I relax a little. I'd much rather be mom to a smart and musical little person than a beautiful flower.

I try not to snatch the tiny referral photo right out of Pat's hands. Ni Qiao Qin is now ten months old, and this picture was taken half her life ago. Wispy dark hair spikes above her fat round face. Bundled in so many layers that her arms stick out on either side, she looks as if she's being prepared for crucifixion. I can't tell if she's trying to smile or work her mouth into a scowl, but the resulting expression is wise, knowing, and slightly challenging. She's a butterball with an attitude.

Pat tries to hand me more papers, but I can't take my eyes off the photo, not so much mesmerized by the sight of my child so much as dismayed, trying to contain my rising alarm, desperate to discern whether she has a neck. It's hard to distinguish any body at all under the bulk of so many layers, the top one a pink hand-knit sweater with orange, white, and black stitchlike stripes. On her collar there's a doll-head pin, round and grinning and lacking a neck, gruesomely reinforcing the illusion that the baby is also missing body parts. Her shoulders practically touch her ears, as if she is suited up to go out for the Yiwu City Social Welfare Institute Football Team.

Pat's trying to explain the process of applying for a visa, but I finally can't stand it. "Are you sure she has a neck?" I interrupt.

"She has a neck," Pat says.

"She's kind of funny looking," I say, aiming for an affectionate tone but striking a dubious one. I am mostly disappointed, having expected my first glimpse of my child's picture to be a dramatic psychic experience. I thought there would be a sign—that she would share a birthday with my mother, or that her name would be mine backward, or that she'd be called "Su Fui," something close to Sophie.

"She has pretty little features," Pat says.

"Are you sure her arms aren't growing out of her ears?" I fight panic.

"Her arms are completely normal," Pat says firmly. I wonder if she is bluffing. How can she know for sure?

I stare, willing myself to experience that lightning-flash moment of irrevocable connection. Surely the awful clothes are grounds for empathy. As children, and I like to imagine somewhat against our wills, my brothers and I wore homemade double-knit polyester turtleneck T-shirts, too-short pants with huge bell-bottoms, and matching overalls covered with big yellow happy faces. We didn't just wear them around the house, either. We went to school and to the mall that way, and to restaurants, and the fact that it was the seventies no longer seems to be much of an excuse.

I examine the baby's expression, the face of this Ni Qiao Qin who I try to think of as Sophie, but it isn't working. She isn't a Sophie, she's a Ni Qiao Qin. And she isn't my daughter, she's just some baby in a Chinese orphanage.

"Do you accept?" Pat asks.

"Yes," I say, unable to picture myself as this baby's mom.

I prop the picture on my steering wheel, puzzling all the way home at the idea that this baby is supposed to accompany me from China and live in my house.

People are always comparing the adoption process to pregnancy, and many women report similar hormonal reactions; some have even been known to lactate. Many joke during the paperwork process that they are trying to conceive; once the dossier goes to China, they announce that they are officially expecting. Others are always telling adoptive parents that we're taking the easy way out. During the long wait and many delays, one pregnant woman says to me, "Now you're getting a little taste of what it's like to have your own."

I grit my teeth, tempted to snap back, "No, you're getting a little taste of what it's like to adopt your own!" By now, I've been waiting the approximate gestation period of three baby elephants, and this smug woman only has to wait nine months or so.

Many adoptive parents compare the referral photo, often faxed and grainy, to the ultrasound photo; the jittery feeling before they meet their babies—or the stomach bug from drinking the water—to labor pains; and the jet lag after the twenty-four-hour return trip to recovery from a C-section.

I resist the pregnancy metaphor. The whole process has been disappointingly aphysical, a matter of producing lots of copies of the same documents stapled, notarized, authenticated, and translated according to rigid rules. The process feels like an intellectual exercise, like getting my Ph.D. or learning a language, not like giving birth.

For weeks, while I pack and wait for travel approval, I stare and stare at the picture of Ni Qiao Qin, trying to decipher the code of her expression, trying to imagine her as a flesh-and-blood baby.

After five weeks of packing, unpacking, making lists, revising them, and repacking, I'm ready to go. I will set out tomorrow carrying a large rolling duffle and a diaper bag and wearing a neck wallet that contains five thousand dollars in the crisp hundred-dollar bills preferred by Chinese officials for the orphanage donation and other fees. The diaper bag is jammed with several pounds of documents and copies in clear plastic covers, labeled "For the Province" and "For the Consulate." Our clothes—my four outfits, Sophie's twelve—are folded tightly and sealed in Ziploc bags.

I have squeezed a can of formula into the duffel, packets of soup mix, oatmeal, and hot chocolate, a big package of diapers, and a small pharmacy of baby drugs. Along with an assortment of baby ibuprofen and acetaminophen and some cotton swabs and some tongue depressors given to me by a doctor friend without any directions about what I might need them for, I've included cream for scabies, medication to prevent the cold sores I get under stress, lice shampoo, and a cream someone recommended for diaper rash that was shelved with the condoms and feminine lubricants. I bought these all at the same time at Wal-Mart, remedies for scabies, herpes, lice, and feminine dryness. My heart thumped as I kept on the lookout for people I knew and willed the clerk to hurry up and bag my purchases. According to lore, people have been fired from my college for lesser rumors than the ones this combination of items might spawn.

I've never packed so efficiently; I will probably never again travel so light. Briefly I wonder if I really need my townhouse full of possessions when I can squeeze three weeks' of necessities for me and a baby into two bags.

I anticipate shedding weight along the way—diapers, wipes, formula, gifts for officials and caretakers, clothing and toys for the orphanage, and underwear. I've packed my rattiest pairs to discard after I wear each one the last time. I also plan to ditch each book as I finish it, in plane seat pockets and hotel rooms; I've heard that Chinese workers are delighted to find English-language material.

Before I leave, I have to do one last thing. I go to see the dean for my annual end-of-the-year evaluation. In the past, the dean has encouraged me to go up for early tenure, which appeals to me; it seems like the only way to stop worrying about the stability of my job and the fickleness of some of my colleagues year after year. But this time, the dean clears his throat and looks embarrassed and finally tells me to hold off on my tenure application. He tells me that I don't have enough support.

"Look, don't worry about it now!" he says. "Go to China and get that baby! You've got plenty of other things to think about."

The next day, I will board a plane, on my way at last to go and get that baby. I will exit a life measured by seconds, minutes, and hours, and enter one measured by clouds, clumps of fog, and vast expanses of sky. Sloping above the black rooftops of houses, forests of evergreen tips, reddish patches of South Carolina earth, rows of trucks in a warehouse lot that resemble carelessly flung strands of pearls, and cars like just so many stitches along seams of highway, I will wait futilely for my anxiety to shrink into silly earthly concerns, toy problems I've left behind, as blurred and irrelevant as the white hum of voices around me.

Instead, the world's weight seems to press against me. I drag all of my burdens from gate to gate at airports, Atlanta to Kansas City to Minneapolis to San Francisco to Shanghai to Beijing, load them on each plane. I am about to become a mom. I am about to lose my job. I am slipping through the invisible boundaries of time zones under a sun that burns brightly, never setting, the possessions that define me all left behind, the roles by which I identify myself thrown into question. I am nowhere, in no time, hanging in space, staring at a picture of a baby who half-frowns, half-smiles, arms outstretched as if poised to take flight.

China

3

A rumor spreads through our travel group as we trudge down the walkways of the stifling Beijing airport teeming with people and board our flight to Hangzhou. I'm too tired to pay much attention, but my cousin Jody reports back to me as we wait to claim our baggage and then board a minivan to speed past rows of camphor: a couple of the babies will be here this evening.

Of course mine's not one of them. If she were, wouldn't I have been told by now? Agency representatives have joined our group of six families, three couples and three single women accompanied by assorted helpers, a sister, parents, and, in my case, Jody. Now we've added a facilitator, two women from the agency's international division, and two U.S. social workers on their way to escort babies from Korea. These professionals will have certainly notified parents who are receiving their children early.

I'm so glad that my baby isn't arriving till tomorrow. Days of touring in the hot sun and hauling heavy bags have taken their toll on me. The muscles that don't downright ache feel shot through with a paralyzing weariness. My lower back blazes, and the parts of my brain that store information and produce emotion seem to have shut down altogether.

The whirlwind tour of Beijing sounded good when I was preparing for the trip, a chance to acquaint myself with the culture and history of my future child's home country. At first, as we gathered around our interpreter at the Forbidden City, I struggled to absorb all of her words. Increasing numbers of impressed and curious Chinese tourists joined our group, listening to our articulate young female guide, with her flawless memory, recite, in fluent English, facts and dates and names of emperors. My traveling companions listened intently, took notes, held up microphones to preserve information on tape, and filmed through the lenses of their camcorders.

I, on the other hand, became distracted by watching children and listening to the foreign words that flowed around me like rivers into seas of sound. Pretty soon I had slinked from the center of our group to the fringes and was posing with the many Chinese tourists who approached and asked to have their pictures taken with me. Young women in uniform hurried over to take their turns, and parents and grandparents sent over small children to stand with me. I was feeling like a movie star—or like the one at Disneyland in the Mickey Mouse costume.

"It's your blond hair," another parent-to-be informed me when our guide concluded one of her lengthy lectures and rushed us past the actual sites. "They're fascinated by blond hair."

This became the pattern of our three days: long, long lectures, then rushing. Me, the only one in the group with multiple advanced degrees, now the bad student, the class airhead, always daydreaming or wandering off from the group. Meals with overflowing mugs of beer or, for those of us abstaining, a few drops of Coke. An outdoor café with the sun beating on us and cranky waiters and spotty tablecloths and greasy food, chicken and greens, rice and soup, goose full of fine bones, the meat delicious after our hours of walking. Visits to Friendship Stores, an enamel factory, more historical sites, more meals at a cool dim hotel with white china, crisp white tablecloths, silverware, and courteous waiters in white dinner jackets. Attendants in the rest rooms who led us to stalls and arranged paper on the seats, then turned on the faucets when we emerged and dusted off our backs while we washed. More historical sites, more long lectures, more rushing, moving so fast through the jam-packed summer palace that it felt like an enforced march along the damply chilly lake, all of us paying so much attention to the babies that they stretched their hands to us and their mothers called out, "Ai yi. Ai yi." This meant *auntie,* our guide told us. It was an honorary title for childless women who took an interest in others' babies.

At the Ming Tombs the guide delivered a fifteen-minute talk on every ar-
tifact behind each glass case of pottery and brocaded pants and silk gowns.
I spaced out. By the time we left, I was vaguely ashamed that I had no earthly idea what exactly the Ming Tombs were, except that dead people, probably emperors, were buried there. I thought of all the people who kept saying I was lucky to escape morning sickness and labor pains. Let *them* take
a three-hour tour along three walls of glass cases in a dimly lighted hall.

I'm tired. I'm grumpy. I'm in no shape to become a mom. I want a hot
shower, some ibuprofen, and a good night's sleep. I hope some others in
the group will get their babies tonight. Maybe the sight of others' babies
will revive my emotion that has been killed off by exhaustion. The other
day we passed around the tiny referral photos with red backgrounds. All
of the other babies were so cute, with distinct little features. My Sophie
Qiaoqin has a more bloblike quality. I've resigned myself to the funniest
looking baby. I expect I'll love her more because she's funny looking.

Tonight I will admire cute babies and rediscover whatever longing
brought me here. I'll play with the babies and build up my anticipation
again. Right now, yearning and anticipation seem preferable, more exciting and less ambiguous, than fulfillment. I want to savor longing, anticipation, and my last night alone.

"The contractions are starting," Pam announces as we gather around
the hotel desk filling out forms and showing passports.

"Wash your knee, Mama, wash your knee, Baba," I hear Paul, one of the
men in our group, murmur. Earlier today, I taught everyone the Chinese
for "I am your mother" and "I am your father," which Paul has slightly
transliterated.

Shiyan, our facilitator, speaks in rapid Chinese to a clerk. I fantasize
about steaming water pounding into the small of my back. I imagine how
the water will loosen my sore, tired muscles and leave me drowsy. I'll take
a long nap before dinner.

Shiyan turns to us. "The Yiwu babies will be here at six," she says
offhandedly. "I'll call your rooms when they arrive."

Startled silence erupts into a hubbub of hugging, babbling, and con-
gratulations. Tears of joy glitter in Brandy's eyes. I want to cry, too. If I do,
I hope that people will mistake my tears for happiness. I do a double take
at my watch. It's already five-thirty.

The rest of my life slips out of my hands.

Pam's eyes fill: her baby won't arrive till tomorrow.

"We don't have any film," Jody says. I accidentally rewound the camera this morning. Our additional film is in the luggage that hasn't been delivered yet. So are all the diapers and baby clothes and toys, the formula and cereal and drugs. I had my ritual all planned out, how tonight I would organize baby clothes into drawers, set up a bottle station in the bathroom, and organize shelves of snacks and toys. Jody and I would bone up a little on babies by reading the photocopies I made from parenting books.

Instead I am rushing to unpack carry-on bags and assess our supplies. My thoughts scatter, come together, fly apart again like the beads in a kaleidoscope shifting into new formations every time I turn around. I heap papers on the bed, fling toothpaste and shampoo onto the bathroom counter, and deposit spare underwear and socks in a drawer.

Jody is irritatingly calm. She borrows film and boils water.

What are we going to do? What does either of us know about taking care of a baby? If I had time, I would panic. I swallow some ibuprofen. If I hurry, maybe I can at least sit immobile for a minute or two, close my eyes, and find a calm, still center, focus the way I do before a difficult presentation or interview.

I stash away my money and passport and sort my documents and will the phone not to ring, not just yet, not for a few more minutes.

The phone rings. I stare in terror at my placid cousin.

The day before I left for China, an acquaintance said, "You mean, you've never taken care of a baby and you're taking along someone who doesn't have children either?"

I babysat infants when I was a teenager—twice. Both screamed nonstop. I'm definitely not a natural, but Jody is close to her niece and nephews.

But I've been worrying ever since my colleague's comments. At tourist sites, Jody didn't even seem to notice the children. She was busy shooting close-ups of carved stones, bamboo-lined roofs and bamboo scaffolding secured by wire, suspension bridges and the summer palace's long promenade, a covered walkway with beams and a ceiling intricately decorated by pictures and patterns. My photos were of smiling, round-cheeked children, no sibling groups, each single child accompanied by one or two doting parents. It was warm out, but the festivity of the May Day holiday and the practice of keeping children covered won out over color coordination or dressing for the weather. One of my pictures shows a little girl in a sheer tulle dress with a purple sash over a heavy red turtleneck and black leggings covered by colorful polka dots. Another captures a child in a flame-retardant pink dress that looks like my childhood Halloween costumes over a yellow and orange striped jersey and Mickey Mouse leggings.

My motives for taking these photos were not pure. I want to someday show them to my daughter when my taste and my habits start to embarrass her. She'll have to feel at least a smidgen of gratitude that I've never dressed her like a typical Chinese child. In turn, many Chinese tourists will giggle with their friends at their pictures of the tall American woman in the baseball cap and two pairs of glasses, large sunglasses covering prescription lenses. "Dragonfly," my Japanese students used to call me, because of my three-tiered eyes.

Despite my secret agenda, I was fascinated by all of the beautiful, pampered children we saw. I searched their faces for clues to what my own child would someday look like. I tried to decide whether I could love each one. The question no longer had much to do with physical appearance, if it ever had; I was mesmerized by how beautiful I found every child, especially the ones with rashes, quirks, and flame-retardant clothes. Yet still I watched them, mystified and terrified at the knowledge that somehow I would need to summon up love for a child I'd never seen.

When I pointed children out to her, Jody just grunted and returned her spellbound attention to the architecture.

When I first asked Jody to accompany me, it was because I knew she'd make a good traveling companion. I didn't think beyond that. Jody and I have roomed together at a zillion family reunions in isolated rural midwestern towns connected somehow to our mothers' childhoods. The prospect of squat toilets and marinated rat on a stick seemed like nothing after some of the midwestern motels we'd stayed at: musty, moldy, with doors requiring brute force to open and air conditioners emitting high-pitched squeals. Carpets that turned the bottoms of socks black, smoke detectors that had been ripped off the wall and stuffed into the nightstand drawer next to the Gideon Bible. Footsteps pounding up and down the halls all night and, sometime before dawn, a group of drunken Shriners test-firing rifles and driving miniature cars into the pool.

For hours each year we hung around dilapidated VFW halls, eating

American cheese and white bread sandwiches and listening to our parents reminisce, relate their most recent consumer complaints, and argue about health care, abortion rights, and the role of government. The only real conflicts stemmed from a competition to one-up each other in denouncing liberals.

My cousins and my older brother and I usually escaped in the evenings to play board games and eat junk food. My cousins always brought lots of big board games with names I could never remember. One required players to make timed lists, like "Things that are cold" in which everything had to start with an *s*. Other people wrote down *sherbet, snow, Siberia, spritzers, salad, Saturn*. I drew a blank and put *socks in the freezer,* which received boos and instant disqualification. In China, thinking back on this game while in the middle of a full-fledged anxiety attack about my impending parenthood, I'm suddenly convinced that it's a sign that Jody lacks flexibility and creativity. I think about how she rolls her eyes when I crave a vegetable or have an allergic reaction or sudden blood-sugar plunge. I conclude, in my fogged half-panic, that I have brought to China the least nurturing person on the planet. But then I remember that that's me.

I recall some game my cousins and I also played, where you weren't limited to a single letter of the alphabet—a relief. I could do that. The category was "Things to Trim a Tree." After the timer buzzed, I listened to everyone's lists: *tinsel, ornaments, candy canes, popcorn, gifts, crèches, lights, ceramic angels*. I hadn't even thought about holiday decorating. I felt like the family psychopath. My list included *garden shears, chain saws, Edward Scissorhands.*

Jody and I have a whole history together, a thousand memories of childhood trips and days at the pool and songs we sang before sleep. She taught me "Great Big Gobs of Greasy Grimy Gopher Guts" and "You Should Not Laugh when a Hearse Goes By (Cause You May Be the Next To Die)." Together when we were children we memorized Morse code and then communicated over holiday dinner tables with our noses: a wiggle for a dot, flared nostrils for a dash. We played Laura Ingalls Wilder, pretending our beds were covered wagons. Jody was the maid of honor at my wedding. And for years we have endured countless family reunion dinners of yet more white bread, overcooked roast beef with slabs of fat, iceberg salad, and speeches honoring the dead and announcing births, except the out-of-wedlock ones, a custom about which I stewed and muttered.

I knew, before we came to China, that Jody would have the stomach for just about anything, but now I see that I have chosen my travel companion for all the wrong reasons. I should have brought some cuddly earthmother friend with many children and grandchildren, except I don't actually have any of those. At least none capable of taking off to a foreign country for two weeks.

"Do you know how to change a diaper?" I ask as we head out the hotel room door.

"Of course," Jody says, loading the camera.

I'm not reassured.

I am the first parent to hit the shadowy doorway of Shiyan's hotel room. Inside, three men jiggle babies on their knees. I hesitate, but Shiyan impatiently ushers me in.

"Ni Qiao Qin," she announces, gesturing at a baby.

My travels so far have made me realize how comparatively new everything in the United States is, from shiny airport floors to fast-food restaurants whose plastic chairs and tables are rarely scuffed or cracked. Here, except for at our hotels, floors are dingy, the paint on walls often dirty and chipped, the furniture threadbare and not fashionable in at least forty years.

My first thought about the baby that a small, smiling man with a mustache holds out to me is that she is not new either.

I mean, I knew she wouldn't be, and I'm okay with that—but she's so big, so real, so fully formed, so loud. The cry that rises to a wail is ear shattering. The baby clutches wildly at the man's shirt, then looks back over her shoulder at me, screaming.

This baby has fat red cheeks and bright quick scared eyes, nothing like the challenging stare of the referral photo. Maybe it's because of that photo that I'm so surprised to find a baby rather than a wise old creature— was I expecting Yoda? She's wearing a T-shirt, a sweatshirt covered with basketballs and footballs, and a pair of yellow overalls with a bunny on the front. The clothes are all made of a coarse kind of polyester that I think has been outlawed in the United States, the kind that if set afire laminates skin. The baby's red-patterned sneakers, several sizes too big, are tied around her ankles with ribbons.

I kneel and talk to her. I say, "Wo shi ni mama."

The caretaker nods approvingly. "Zhe shi ni mama," he says.

I go on murmuring in a soothing voice, only increasing the baby's suspicion and anger. She tightens her grip on the man and notches up the volume.

The caretaker smiles apologetically. He thrusts her toward me and her scream escalates, hitting a new note: terror.

I sit on the bed and pat the place beside me. It's okay with me if the caretaker and I just sit there. The baby can get used to me gradually. I talk and talk, gently, reassuringly, repeating over and over, "I'm your mommy. Wo shi ni mama."

Flashbulbs pop around us. The room has slowly filled, two couples and one other single woman accepting their own serene babies and posing with them. Over the low roar of voices arch the cries of this baby, the one who's supposed to be my daughter.

The caretaker looks anxious, as if he fears I won't want the baby if this keeps on. He abruptly extricates her and dumps her in my lap. She reaches after him, straining desperately toward the only familiarity in the room, but he squeezes my hand and moves away, his expression sad but determined.

"He used to take her home to visit his family," Joy from the agency tells me.

"Get her a toy," Shiyan says. "Try some Cheerios."

Everyone else is smiling and laughing and passing their babies back and forth and trying to act as if my baby isn't making a scene.

The toys and Cheerios and bottles and formula are in my luggage, en route from the airport.

Anyway, I can't believe that rattles or cereal are going to trick the grief out of this baby.

I carry her away from the chaos, into the hall that echoes with her cries. In our room, I gently bounce her and talk and sing. My back and shoulders burn. The noise drills through my eardrums. I've found noise annoying before—shrieking children, rock music thumping on the other side of apartment walls. I've started at the sound of thunder so close the windows vibrate, seen how a car stereo passing on the street can pulsate so forcefully that its bass tinkles glasses in the kitchen cupboard. I know that sound can do damage, can function as a weapon, but I've never before experienced it as a steady, continuous pain.

What kind of mother will I be, that already the sound of my child's voice hurts?

When her face smooths for just an instant now and then, when she has no choice but to pause for a breath, I see that Pat was right: this baby has pretty little features—distinctively beautiful features. And such bright eyes and such lungs. Smart and musical—no wonder.

This is what I wanted, right? Passion, fervor, tenacity.

I sway, I sing, she screams.

I walk her up and down the hall. She screams.

The luggage arrives. Jody rustles up toys, cereal, formula, and bottles, diapers, cotton outfits. This baby will not be distracted. When we try to change her into softer, cooler clothes, she bellows at us with all the unsettling vigor of a siren wailing through the night.

I sing whatever comes to mind. A song I remember from third grade music class called "Land of the Silver Birch" and another one from sixth grade choir called "Thou Art Groovy." "The Star Spangled Banner" and "Home on the Range" and "Amazing Grace" and "Great Big Gobs of Greasy Grimy Gopher Guts." She screams, I persist.

> Oh, she came from Yiwu, China
> With a set of tiny knees
> Oh she'll come to South Carolina
> Oh my true child for to be.
> Oh, my Sophie, oh don't you cry my babe
> You're going to South Carolina for to be a McCabe.

Sheer exhaustion or, at the very least, hoarseness, ought to be overtaking this baby by now. But she shows no signs of losing her voice or winding down.

Ready to concede defeat, I launch a last-ditch effort: the theme song from *Gilligan's Island*. After a couple of lines, Jody joins in.

And then, right in the middle of the story of the *Minnow*'s ill-fated three-hour tour, Sophie Qiaoqin abruptly goes silent. And smiles.

Jody stays with the baby while I deliver my gifts for the orphanage officials to Shiyan. I've followed agency directions, bringing T-shirts and pens from my college. Shiyan raises her eyebrows as if my offerings are spectacularly tacky.

Shiyan is a tall, beautiful woman of some sort of Asian ancestry, with the oversized features of a model and the efficient bearing of a lawyer.

Since meeting her, I've felt as if I were being sized up, as if she's figured out that, unlike most agency employees and clients, I'm pro-choice, I don't eschew Halloween as a pagan holiday, and I'm more likely to become a lesbian than marry a Promise Keeper. A smile frequently curls Shiyan's lip but doesn't reach her eyes when she looks at me, as if she knows that I am the sort of person who dreaded meeting my child early.

Shiyan gives me some photos—a group shot of orphanage caretakers, a picture of the building where my baby lived, and a snapshot of unfamiliar babies in walkers tooling around a large bare room.

Shiyan also has some instructions for me: Be sure to cover the baby well. Chinese babies don't like to be cold. And be sure that you don't let Jody hold or feed her for a few days. You don't want her to bond with Jody.

This very minute, Jody is holding and feeding the baby. Of course I want the baby to bond with Jody. Can't healthy children form all kinds of bonds?

Sophie Qiaoqin wakes at three in the morning and wants to play. I let her lie on my bed. I surround her with toys. She shakes rattles in both fists, beats them against the mattress, and laughs.

Giving her toys was obviously a mistake—we're up the rest of the night. But this angry, loud baby has transformed into a maniacally happy one, and although I know that these emotions are just the other side of grief's coin, I can't bear to disrupt them.

At the Office of Civil Affairs, we troop into a room with rows of long tables, as brown-gray dreary as a factory warehouse except for the Christmas bulbs strung along the edges of the ceiling. The caretakers hover in the background while we write essays about why we want to adopt a baby. We check off whether we like the baby we've been offered, yes or no. Then we fingerprint the pages, add red baby footprints, and sign agreements never to abandon or abuse our children.

Sophie Qiaoqin's eyes brighten at the sight of her caretaker. I carry her over. He tickles her and blows raspberries on her cheek and she giggles, a wonderful baby giggle. She comes back to me without a fuss, but her attitude is more resignation than willingness.

At my request, Shiyan joins us to translate an interview with an orphanage official and the caretaker. She keeps glancing at her watch and snapping out comments in Chinese to passing officials. I ask about the babies' schedules and meals.

The answers delivered by a solemn older man are vague. The caretaker sits by beaming, saying little. It's evident from the flat spot on my baby's head that she spent a lot of time in a crib, although the official says that the babies played in walkers much of the time. The man emphasizes this and the fact that the babies drank milk, as if he expects such information to be pleasing. I understand that these are the things that most Americans wish to hear.

Was there a note with her when she was found? I ask.

The caretaker talks for a long time. Shiyan responds. He answers her. She finally tells me that there was a note, but I can't see it. The files will be kept for seventy years. My child can access hers if she wants to someday.

I try to get Shiyan to ask whether the note says anything more than a date of birth. She looks at me impatiently and refuses to translate.

"Ask if there's anything I should tell her from you," I say. I hope for some words of affection, something to remind my baby that she mattered to someone the first few months of her life.

"Thank you for adopting her," Shiyan translates, abruptly ending the interview as she becomes distracted by apparently more pressing duties. She races across the room, yelling to an official in rapid Chinese.

The caretaker makes playful faces at my baby. She radiates.

Sue from the agency is sitting at the back of the room, in sunlight, looking bored. I ask her about the note. How can I see it or obtain a copy?

The head of the agency's international division, Sue has been uncommunicative from the start, seeming oddly reluctant to update or reassure me or answer questions during the paperwork and waiting process, speaking to me with an abruptness that I wrote off as a cross between midwestern reticence and East Coast terseness.

Later, I will find out that the notes may be as mythical as the milk the babies drank and the floors they played on for hours every day, that notes are one more thing that Americans expect. But I'll never know this for sure, or why Sue squints up at me, not answering, lips pursed like she's blowing invisible smoke into my face.

Steaming, I return to my baby. What is wrong with these people? Do they suspect that my job is unstable? Are they put off because I'm single but unlike the other single women, I don't constantly point out that my home may not be ideal since I lack a husband, but it beats an orphanage? Do they disapprove because, unlike other group members, I'm not always referring to the Lord's plan for my life? Do they think I'm gay, the issue that repeatedly arose during the paperwork process? Or maybe they are easily offended. I'm always inadvertently offending those who are more conservative. I think back. Was it a conjecture I made about Freud's theory of penis envy being based on interviews with Chinese women who had to use squat toilets?

I have such a horrible tendency to blurt out the unmentionable and an endless capacity to be surprised by people's scandalized responses. More than once I've created consternation in my own family when I made a feminist comment or brought up a subject not suitable for polite company. Like at a reunion where we were celebrating an aunt and uncle's wedding anniversary. "Oh, my God, today's *my* fifteenth wedding anniversary," I exclaimed, having just realized it. The room fell silent and gazes swept the floor with discomfort and pity, strange to me when I'd been divorced for years and didn't see any point in pretending to erase my marriage from memory. But maybe, I consoled myself, everyone's reaction was just shock and disapproval at my habit of taking the Lord's name in vain.

I don't have time to ponder what in the world has offended the agency people. Sophie's mood plummets again as the day goes by and all of my attention returns to her. I'm just grateful to have had a buffer and advocate in my warm, kind social worker, Pat. The social workers who are with us now remind me of her, their gentle wisdom creating a calming presence. They stand by, never offering advice unless it's couched in the most supportive of terms, take Sophie from me when I need a break and give her back the second my guilt takes over, and take pictures when we're all too preoccupied to remember to do so. So when Shiyan scrutinizes me with open disdain, when Sue looks at me as if I am a bug she'd like to flick off her sleeve, I shrug it off, impatient with their rudeness. I have a fussy baby to attend to.

Most of the babies respond to their recent separation trauma with glazed eyes and zombie lethargy. What at first appeared to be calm, adaptable temperaments simply prove to be quieter responses than Sophie's to shock and grief. Pam's Lily trembles visibly much of the time. The other parents worry about their babies' constipation. Sophie is opposite in every way: squirmy, rowdy, and vocal, always demanding my full attention and suffering from relentless diarrhea. Other parents cast pitying looks at me, but I secretly feel smug. I know I have the best baby, the smartest, most sensitive, most curious, and most beautiful.

And I'm not biased: Jody agrees with me.

I can hardly believe that this woman is my cousin. I've always thought of her as a little bossy and stubborn, a little unyielding, and, in the words of one of my friends, as "emotionally independent," largely lacking interest in what others think of her.

With my baby, Jody is characteristically practical and efficient, yet she can also stand swaying and humming for a solid hour, calming the baby when I can't, holding out until she drops off to sleep.

Who knew that Jody had the patience to outlast such a determined baby? I have never seen this side of my cousin; she can whip off one diaper and secure another in record time and can, with competent tenderness, spoon cereal into a baby's mouth, catching the overflow that dribbles down her chin with expert swipes. Jody has always been slightly impatient and endlessly steady, without my more mercurial temperament, my extremes of impatience, frustration, or giddiness, and yet I realize that I've never seen her in love before, so nakedly defenseless in the presence of another human being.

The way Jody lights up around Sophie, sometimes I'm afraid that my baby will like Jody better than she likes me. Sometimes I'm even afraid that Jody is going to kidnap Sophie or worse, file for custody. Any judge will see that she's the capable one.

Like four of the other babies, Sophie suffers from congestion and a cough. Then there's her diarrhea, and the rashes on her face and legs seem to be spreading. I wonder if she is lactose intolerant. Milk products made me sick for much of my life. As a child and teenager, I was embarrassed at the sudden onslaughts of stomach cramps and diarrhea, but it wasn't till my early thirties that I stumbled upon the explanation and learned that the incidence of lactose intolerance is even higher among nonwhites. I have been prepared to note the signs in my child, yet they are so blatant that I distrust my amateur diagnosis. If it were that simple, wouldn't a professional already have identified the reason for the rash and diarrhea?

The orphanage representative told me that all the babies drank milk, but I know from my own experience that Americans are fanatical about milk, that our image of a healthy child is one with big bones, gleaming straight teeth, and a milk mustache. Since milk is less readily available and more expensive in China, it's possible that the babies didn't really drink milk formula till recently, soon before they were brought to us.

But still. By the time I met Sophie Qiaoqin, her cheeks were blooming with color. "Rosy cheeks," everyone says approvingly. Yet her cheeks flame brighter all the time, and I'm not sure that the brightness is a sign of health.

I push aside my doubts. I'm just a nervous new mommy, overreacting.

The babies cough and sneeze and breathe laboriously, so Shiyan arranges an excursion to the children's hospital. She escorts us off the bus and whisks us past a TCBY with gold letters in the window spelling out "Merry Christmas."

"The Country's Best Yogurt," says the sign under the TCBY logo. Which country? I wonder.

We parade into a gymlike waiting area with rows of black molded plastic chairs bolted to the concrete floor, no conversational groupings of soft furniture or tables heaped with magazines common to American waiting rooms. A smell—gasoline?—permeates the building. I wonder if it used to be an auto shop.

At a screened window, Shiyan talks in rapid Chinese before she collects our money. I pay six yuan per doctor and one yuan for a lab test—twelve yuan, about $1.50—so that Sophie can see a dermatologist and an ear, nose, and throat doctor. Shiyan hustles us upstairs past another waiting room, right into an examining room. We line up to show our babies to the doctor.

The ear, nose, and throat specialist listens to Sophie's chest and back, pulls a tongue depressor out of a jar, finishes with it, and tosses it into what I would swear is the same jar. Jody will assure me later that it isn't.

The doctor diagnoses an upper respiratory infection and prescribes an antibiotic along with cough medicine containing an antihistamine.

Shiyan conducts us into the upstairs waiting room. At the far end, in a child's play area, two babies leap around in jumper saucers, weird frenzied motion in a room full of heavy-lidded mothers slumped in seats as if they've been waiting a long, long time. The same song repeats again and again, an endless loop of children singing "Old McDonald Had a Farm" in Chinese. The only word I recognize is "EIEIO."

Jody delivers one of Sophie's dirty diapers to the lab for tests, and Shiyan marches us through hallways to a second doctor.

Sophie squirms in my arms, pushing against their limits in her never-abating quest to follow all motion in the room. She babbles nonstop, then howls, eyes wild with fear as the second doctor traces the redness in her cheeks and the dry skin on her legs. He prescribes two creams.

Based on Sophie's stool sample, a third doctor prescribes two diarrhea drugs.

I now have instructions to administer six different prescription medications. I wonder if the doctors have considered lactose intolerance.

I ask Shiyan, whose only answer is raised eyebrows, as if to ask where I earned *my* medical degree.

We return downstairs to wait for the other parents and babies. Jody and I sink into plastic chairs, me trying to keep a grip on Sophie as she wriggles and twists. A Chinese woman drops down beside us, slings her son over her knee, yanks down his pants, and takes his temperature rectally. The boy, about five or six, lies limp as a sack of rice, gazing at me with the sad eyes of a feverish child.

We finally leave Teresa and Paul at the hospital. Bridget has pneumonia and the doctor orders penicillin injections. Paul and Teresa tell us later about a row of children receiving intravenous injections; they were told that IVs were the Chinese's first choice over oral medication or shots. The two of them took one look at the scattered bloody pillows and stained sheets and insisted on a series of shots, for which they have to return twice a day.

That evening, Sophie drops off in her spread-eagled, about-to-be-crucified position familiar from her referral photo, which must have been taken right before she dozed off or right as she was waking. I wonder if the flash scared her, and who was there to comfort her.

I've barely slept or eaten the last two days, and as I sit and watch her sleep, it's the first time both of us have been at ease together. Sophie clutches rattles and stacking cups in her fists, hanging on tight even in sleep. I wonder if I will ever learn to feel peaceful when she is awake.

Jody has gone downstairs to e-mail our parents to let them know that we have the baby and that she is beautiful. I think I ought to get up and find a snack, but rummaging through the luggage sounds like a lot of work. Moving at all sounds like a lot of work. Eating, showering, washing bottles—every task seems to take spectacular effort. Every morning, I lug Sophie down the row of big covered silver bowls in the hotel restaurant, hash browns and bacon and waffles, noodles and dim sum and congee, runny scrambled eggs and cereal labeled "Frosted Flacks." Nothing appeals to me enough to wrestle with Sophie so that I can get a few bites down.

At lunches, she grabs at the turntable and the water glasses and the silverware and the napkins. Bleakly, I watch the food go by, chicken, beef, celery, and tofu, greens and dumplings with duck, bowls of soup and plates of rice, and at every meal, a plate heaped high with saltless french fries, accompanied by a sweet spicy ketchup. If I had more energy, I'd be embarrassed at the Chinese conception of Americans as people who can't get through a meal without french fries.

At this rate, I think, I will lose more than the ten pounds typical for adoptive parents in China. But even though hunger gnaws at me and I fantasize about the smell, the taste of food, I lie back on my bed and listen, happily, to the silence.

There's a sharp rap on the door. I scramble up and jerk it open before the noise wakes Sophie. It's Shiyan, delivering Sophie's medicine. She ignores me when I gesture at the sleeping baby, except for raised eyebrows and a sigh at my naïveté, as if I'm too thick or inexperienced to understand that awakened babies eventually go back to sleep. On the bed she spreads out bags and tubes, powders and creams, loudly reviewing the directions.

Sophie wakes with a start and bellows, huge tears leaking from her eyes. I restrain myself from showing Shiyan my exasperation.

Jody takes charge of measuring drugs into Sophie's formula three times a day. As she washes bottles and mixes formula from the boiled water we've been collecting in empty bottles, as she measures a dropper of this and a little waxed paper packet of that, as she mutters "Eye of newt and toe of frog" and then presents me with another bottle of the magic potion, I am grateful and relieved. Jody's calm efficiency means that all I have to do is feed the baby and that's what I desperately need right now, to do only what is essential and get sleep.

But after Sophie starts her prescriptions, she seems worse. The rash spreads higher and wider, flushing her whole face. Her diapers are a mess all the time. She writhes constantly and tugs at her shirt, plucking at the cloth around her tummy. She won't nap. She fights sleep with a loud and agitated babbling, giving in to drowsiness only for brief intervals on the bus. Even at night she catnaps, waking every two hours like a much younger baby, Jody observes. I take her word for it.

On the third day, we return to the Office of Civil Affairs and are shown to a beautiful boardroom with thick red carpet and a round oak table. I vaguely remember a streamlined life, everything I needed contained in a purse or briefcase, as organized and businesslike as the furniture in this room. Within seconds, the floor and chairs and table are strewn with

Snugglies, diaper bags, cameras, toys, and parents chatting and jiggling babies while they fumble for film or wipes or pens.

"Brandy and Gina?" A woman in a silk dress beckons them to the front of the room and launches into Chinese. The rest of us half-attend to the proceedings as we dig through bags, load film, and retrieve the toys our babies throw onto the floor. A second woman begins to translate the first woman's words. "This is now your baby," she says.

There's a communal intake of breath. Heads lift, the room falls silent, and tears shine in everyone's eyes. The women pass Brandy a certificate and a stuffed panda bear. Someone has the presence of mind to take a picture.

We wait solemnly for our turns, and one by one, the babies are pronounced ours. The babies are less reverent. Sophie and Gina keep grabbing their adoption decrees and throwing them on the floor.

Around the corner at the notary office, we spread our gear all over another beautiful room, this time with a walnut table and oversized leather chairs. Otherwise, the setting is less formal, smelling of varnish and sawdust, a karaoke set pushed into a corner. A nearby drill drowns out our attempts at conversation.

We fill out more papers, promising not to abandon our children and to take good care of them.

Sophie bobs and mutters to keep herself awake. The medication seems to make her drowsy, but she fights sleep like crazy.

Back in the hotel room, she plays and whines. Lying on the bed surrounded by stacking cups, she flings her arms and tries to roll over. Then she konks out again.

When I take antihistamines, I get wired rather than knocked out by them. They leave me exhausted but with a buzz so that no matter how much I yearn for sleep, my brain just keeps humming along. I know other people who respond like this, too. Could this be Sophie's problem?

Then I scold myself for projecting my own idiosyncrasies onto this baby. Yeah, right—she's both lactose intolerant *and* adversely affected by antihistamines. I'm doing what I swore I'd never do, trying to make this baby into a carbon copy of myself.

She's been asleep for only a few minutes when it's time for a tour of a silk factory. Reluctantly, we head off to the bus again. I tell Jody my suspicions about Sophie.

"Her system's just getting used to the formula and the medications," Jody says.

We pass a glass case of silkworms, then move on into the factory, but the drone and clack of machinery is deafening. I carry Sophie out to the silk shop.

There, a woman coos and gestures to hold the baby. Uneasily, I allow her to take Sophie from me. Sophie screws up her face. I hover anxiously while her eyes remain on me. She doesn't fuss, but she doesn't look very happy, either.

The woman strides away. Over her shoulder, I catch a glimpse of Sophie's terrified face. I dash over to retrieve her.

Sophie holds her arms out to me.

This baby wants me. It's me she reaches for. I'm astonished.

For the last few days, taking care of a sick baby I barely know, this sad angry baby who cries and screams and rarely sleeps, I've braced myself to do what needs to be done. My weary journal entries, I will realize later, contain the word *scream* twenty-five times so far, with additional references to yelling, hollering, bellowing, and shrieking. I've felt fleeting tenderness that suggests the possibility of love; I've registered affection that could bloom into wonder and delight. Mostly, though, I've plowed on sleeplessly, doggedly, one task at a time.

And then this baby reaches for me and no one else, and it dawns on me that no matter how unsure of my feelings I am and despite my frequent failure to calm her and my total ignorance about babies and Jody's greater ease and their obvious mutual adoration, I am now Sophie's.

For some mysterious reason, she has claimed me as her own.

We return to the hotel after a few more errands—back to the notary to sign more papers, a stop at the passport office so that officials can match our babies' pictures and faces.

Sophie fusses, rubs her eyes, and tugs at her hair—anything not to sleep. Jody goes down to check the e-mail and answer a message from her parents. Mine have not responded to the last one Jody sent. I wonder if they feel left out because Jody is here instead of them. Or maybe they weren't sure whether we'd be checking our messages.

Sophie never does sleep. I pace, hold her, rock her, sing, try to soothe, fight my own despair. And then Sophie discovers her tongue.

When Jody comes back, I show her. "Where's your tongue?" I say, and looking pleased with herself, Sophie pokes it out at Jody.

For a couple of hours, Sophie reveals her tongue on command, and I talk to her. "Ba," I say, over and over, working my way through the four tones.

Sophie laughs and says it back: "Ba! Ba!"

"Baba," I try.

"Baba," she replies, and it feels as if we're communicating, using the first Chinese I learned from Ping Ping.

By evening Sophie is tormented by fatigue. She digs her fists into her eyes and yanks at fistfuls of hair while emitting banshee yells. Every now and then she works up the energy for a good, long, piercing scream.

Jody and I take turns walking, talking, singing, jiggling, swaying.

Sophie's head droops against Jody's collarbone. Her eyes close. My heart swoops up like a bird, light with hope, then relief. Sophie's eyes fly open. She yells.

Jody and I exchange defeated looks.

Finally Sophie lays her head down on Jody's shoulder.

Her eyes fall shut.

Jody eases her into the crib.

It's eight-thirty. It feels like midnight. Jody and I scramble for our pajamas and toothbrushes. We bound into our beds and snap out lights. Everything inside my head goes black.

At one-thirty, Sophie howls. Her diaper is a mess.

My throat has the raw, dry feeling that precedes a cold. My head feels woozy. Sophie's stomach gurgles. She plucks at her onesie.

That's it. I'm going to switch her from milk to soy.

In the morning, Sophie stares up at me from her crib, eyes wide open and bright. She thrashes, pounds her fists, pokes out her tongue, scissors her legs, gleefully dances like a prisoner just released from constraints. Which is what it must feel like to a baby who spent her first few months in a crib bound tightly in warm clothes, now released into a world full of noise and color and movement where she can fully inhabit her body.

"Ba," she calls to me. It's the first time she's seemed more eager than scared about what's ahead.

"Ba," I sing back to her, taking wing on a surge of the joy I was afraid I'd lost.

She's starved, so I give her one more bottle of milk formula. From now on, though, it's soy, I announce.

Jody protests. She's already prepared another bottle of milk, complete with Sophie's cocktail of drugs.

I'm so certain about my decision that I pour it out.

"Ba," I say to Sophie in the four tones, and she smiles, and then we are saying it back and forth again, our first inside joke.

We start the morning at a tourist attraction called the Dragon Cave. We pass the ubiquitous vendors whose hands shoot out from every side, offering Mao hats and panda quilts and photographic books and Hard Rock Cafe T-shirts. I'm feeling so much better today, I consider flipping through a photographic book and returning it to a vendor just so I can say, "Here is the pictorial I borrowed" in Chinese.

Our guide rushes us along efficiently as if the vendors are merely thorny branches we must occasionally swerve to avoid. Soon we arrive at quiet paths bordered by native plants, a stage area where musicians play traditional instruments, and another one where singers demonstrate Chinese opera. I'm so distracted, making kissy faces at Sophie, I don't get around to reading the signs like my fellow new parents, who seem capable of actual conversation about bamboo and jasmine and monkey grass, able to focus because their babies are so comparatively subdued.

Between grief and antihistamines, they have become an oddly blank, silent bunch of babies. Lily the long-legged baby still shivers a little, although Pam wears her in the Snugli at all times, securely up next to her. Bridget remains sick and unresponsive, Victoria and Rebecca so dazed that we all pause with wonder when Terry tickles Rebecca and she giggles. Only Gina, the baby whose calm mom, Brandy, has traveled the world, seems unfazed by all the transitions, as adventurous as Brandy is.

Sophie is the problem child of the group, the noisy, bouncy, aggressive, demanding one, the one most likely to be diagnosed as hyperactive. I can't focus on anything but her. I try to read a sign listing traditional Chinese indicators of good fortune. There's something about a good career and a baby boy.

I turn back to my baby girl.

All of the moms pose with our babies on a bench while the dads and helpers take pictures. Suddenly there's a row of Chinese three deep snapping photos, flashbulbs popping everywhere.

On a cruise around West Lake, I try to relax. The lake is misty and postcard-beautiful, willows sweeping the water, slow boats meandering by, mountains and skyline hazy in the distance. I stay down in the cabin, envying the social workers and agency employees sprawled out up on the deck, sunning their bare legs. I close my eyes and imagine sleeping for a long time, gently rocked over the water.

Jody squeals and leaps up. Liquid poop trickles down Sophie's legs.

The boat docks. Everyone else rises and files out. I lay Sophie on a bench and gingerly remove the dirty diaper and soiled pants. She screams, red-faced with fury at this new discomfort. Her voice carries across the water. I pat her tummy and murmur to her, trying not to jostle her by rushing. Besides, we have no change of clothes. I'm trying to minimize the mess.

"Hurry up." Shiyan backtracks down to the cabin and stands staring at us but offers no help. We are the only ones left on the boat.

I pass Jody the diaper bag and rise to dispose of the diaper. Jody shoves the new one under Sophie and tapes it shut. Sophie wails. I seal the pants in a plastic bag with one hand while patting Sophie with the other.

"Pick her up," Shiyan snaps at me.

Obediently, I abandon my task and pick up the baby, who's too worked up to stop now.

"Put pants on her," Shiyan says. "Chinese babies need to be kept warm."

I don't point out that Sophie's pants are ruined. I don't point out that it is ninety degrees. I let Shiyan herd us off the boat.

"You would never be able to manage without Jody," Shiyan says scornfully.

It's only by a miracle that I don't burst into tears. I take refuge in my bus seat. I'm mad at myself for letting Shiyan get to me. I fight not to cry. My head spins, still light from the beginning of a cold.

We bump along narrow roads between fields of tea and large houses under construction, homes for tea farmers. I clutch Sophie close to me, pitying her for landing such a hopelessly unfit mother. She falls asleep.

When everyone else goes to look at tea leaves, I stay on the bus with my sleeping baby and my misery. I watch Sophie's smooth, dreaming face. Her slow breath is humid against my hands.

Screw Shiyan, I think.

I trail the group into a building for the tea ceremony. Sophie wakes, cheerful. I settle along the wall, where Sophie throws her rattle on the floor, then scoots over to stare at it lying there.

Her eyes widen: she's thrown her toy out of sight, yet there it is, it still exists.

Object permanence. I still have trouble with the concept. I'm often amazed to find keys or papers still in drawers where I put them months before. I'm sometimes startled to run into towns right where the map said they would be. I remember once, years ago, I returned to my childhood home, deserted now but never cleared out. Staying there with friends, I kept discovering things I'd forgotten. A dust-choked child's keyboard with the notes all labeled, a cracked dulcimer, a case with a broken clarinet nestled in its velvet hollows. Downstairs a friend sat down at the black upright piano, not tuned in years. She fingered its keys, picking out melodies, and the words to songs I thought I'd forgotten tumbled out, still there, after all.

My life has felt so temporary for so long, whatever belief I ever had in permanence of any kind has faded. And now here I am, unsuited for parenthood, perhaps, but this baby's mom forever.

Fierce tears threaten, grateful ones.

Screw Shiyan. This baby is mine.

The social workers, those kind women from regional offices who remind me so much of Pat, keep picking up Sophie's toys. Sophie is newly delighted by the attention. She starts throwing her rattle just so that people will retrieve it for her.

A woman in traditional dress, a flowered silk gown, talks about green tea. She pours a little to smell, then a little more to admire, and finally fills our cups and urges us to drink the tea and eat the leaves. The heat feels good on my throat, soothing the soreness.

Sophie tosses her rattle, accepts it back, releases it again. She loves this game. And I remember how surprised I was that day long ago when I found all those abandoned musical instruments right where we'd left them, how surprised I was that I'd never really forgotten words to old songs. My friends and I gathered around the piano, scolding the loves who'd done us wrong, rejoicing that wretches like us were saved.

After I borrow soy formula, Sophie continues to fuss but there are no more diarrhea episodes. Late in the afternoon, Jody studies Sophie as she cries and whines. Thoughtfully, Jody mixes some cereal.

The baby's mouth drops open for each spoonful. I mix another bowl, then another.

"I think we've been starving this baby," Jody says.

My once-tough and nonchalant cousin keeps scooping up spoonfuls of runny rice cereal. It accumulates on Sophie's chin until she resembles a Santa Claus impersonator. I wonder again how I could have known Jody all my life and never seen this gentle, vulnerable person who is so calm and sure with babies, whose whole face softens when she looks at Sophie.

I wonder if Jody has ever considered adopting a baby.

By evening, the soy formula is working like magic. Sophie stops tugging at her clothes. Her stomach quiets. Now that she's retaining food, she gulps down formula and wants more, chows down on helping after helping of cereal.

How could the solution have been so simple? Why didn't I trust my instincts in the first place?

But Sophie still won't nap. She digs her fists into her eyes, rubbing, rubbing. She bangs her stacking cups together. She pulls on her hair.

Jody stays with her when I go to wrap up the paperwork. We pick up red People's Republic of China passports with the babies' referral pictures. Then, at the notary office, Shiyan helps distribute newly glued booklets of documents for us to proofread.

First, adoption decrees, in Chinese with an English translation. We murmur to each other and ask Shiyan questions as we turn pages. Someone clicks a ballpoint pen. Papers shuffle. Next is the birth certificate. I skim it and go on to the third document.

Certificate of abandonment, it says.

The room goes still as one by one, each new parent reaches this document.

Ni Qiao Qin was found at the Chingxi Police Station in Yiwu on the day of her birth, says the statement in my hands.

My eyes film over.

"Where?" someone asks, and then we are answering,

"The police station steps."

"A farmer's market."

"The door of Yiwu Welfare Institute."

Silence falls again. I picture the baby, my baby, a newborn bundled up and squalling on a concrete step, a note pinned to her with a hastily scrawled birth date. I try to imagine the birth mother stealing away, leaving behind a baby that came from her body, that looks like her, a baby that she will never see again.

Maybe the woman, this first mother, already had a child, maybe she was holding out for a boy to support her in her old age, maybe she was young or poor or had failed to get government permission to have a baby.

Many of our little girls will grow up on the other side of the world from biological siblings, especially from brothers. I imagine a beautiful bright-eyed boy that looks like my baby. I imagine a mother who is like my child, witty, moody, stubborn, resilient, a woman whose face shares the beauty of my baby's, a woman with a quick mind, flaring temper, and tender heart. I can't believe it wasn't a wrenching act to give up this baby girl no matter what the circumstances, that this still unfathomable gift I've received won't always be someone else's unfathomable loss.

Shiyan passes out envelopes for our documents. I lay mine on the table, envisioning the man who stumbled across my baby early one morning, a police officer reporting to work, accustomed to finding babies on the station steps. My baby lies keening with her magnificent lungs. I imagine how the man cradles her and she quiets, and somehow, even in the unfocused eyes of a newborn, he sees the sharpness of her curiosity. As he holds her she starts up her crooning that sounds like singing.

Qiao Qin: smart and musical.

"Put the documents in the envelope," Shiyan says sharply.

I raise my head to stare at her. I feel like a child, reprimanded for daydreaming at school, but I am not a child. I am sick of Shiyan's rudeness and insensitivity. I narrow my gaze, giving her my best evil eye, staring her down. She shifts and looks away.

I try not to laugh. I have regressed. This was my elementary school strategy for confronting bullies, never shouting or threatening, just summoning up my own determined scorn.

Back at the hotel, Sophie's awake and delivering shrill screams at random intervals.

"She's just saying 'I'm here,'" Jody translates with weary affection. "'In case you forgot, I'm still here.'"

I don't guess that her presence in the world was reinforced much in an orphanage. Is her voice, so grating, so piercing, so painful when she wants it to be, the reason that she looks well-nourished and hopeful, like someone who hasn't given up the possibility of having an effect on the world around her?

Maybe she's so noisy because of the antihistamines, or maybe she just needs to assert her presence against the obliteration of sleep and a seemingly indifferent universe. I grit my teeth and tell myself this every time she screams.

Every scream is a file scraping away my sanity, an ache threatening to split my forehead from the inside out, a sharp blade knifing through my abdomen. I wonder if Chinese supermarkets sell earplugs.

We walk to the supermarket later, not for earplugs but for soy formula. A tiny, dirty girl follows us, holding out a cup.

"Mo-ney," she says. "Mo-ney."

Jody and I glance at each other. The girl is barely bigger than Sophie, barely out of toddlerhood, and her shrewd eyes and quick wiry movements seem incongruous with her size.

Passersby cast us puzzled glances as we proceed down the street, me carrying Sophie, the little girl darting around us. My baby is heavy and my back hurts and I haven't had a good night's sleep in ages and I know there is nothing more I can do right now. I am still new enough at this to feel anguished and helpless that I can't save anyone, can't change the world. I'm afraid even to offer a few coins lest we find ourselves knee deep in small hungry children.

The little girl falls back, giving up on us. I look at Sophie with bleary eyes and realize the reason we've been attracting strange stares.

Sophie clutches a stacking cup in each fist, as if she too is begging for coins.

The next day is the worst yet. Sophie's digestive problems remain completely cleared up. But she's even more hyper, crazed and frantic, louder than ever, bashing herself constantly with rattles and cups.

I was right about the lactose intolerance. Maybe I am also right about the antihistamines. But she still has a cough and congestion. How can I take it on myself to deny her medication?

I'm sucking zinc lozenges and swallowing huge doses of the echinacea my friend Claudia sent with me. My throat still aches. I can't breathe. I can't remember quite why I ever wanted to come to China and adopt a baby.

We take the bus to a Buddhist temple, thirteen parents and helpers with four placid, drugged babies, cheerful, adaptable Gina, and Sophie. She protests at the top of her lungs and kicks when I lower her into a stroller, a baby carrier, or a high chair. Unless we hold her at all times, she complains, tirelessly shrill. Other parents clench their teeth, their smiles strained.

The heat is sweltering. We walk and walk past the usual booths of T-shirts and postcards. My lower back feels like it might cave in after days of supporting the extra weight of sixteen squirming pounds and of enduring my gymnastics to hang on to her. I trail the group from temple to temple, watching worshipers bearing incense and bowing in rapid succession at the feet of huge gold Buddhas.

My despair steeps the air around me like tea in water, darkening with each passing hour. I sit mutely through lunch, not eating because eating is too much work while Sophie grabs at my plate, rips the plastic tablecloth, and opens all the paper packets of chopsticks within her reach. I shove things out of her way, narrowly averting injuries and destruction.

All afternoon I pace around the hotel, hauling with me this baby who will not sleep and hollers if I stop to rest. Down to the basement bowling alley, through gift shops, up and down in the mirrored elevator. I stare at the sagging woman whose eyes are weary and hopeless, at the bright-eyed baby she hoists. The baby tugs her hair and gathers her breath for another series of screams.

Could that woman be me? Could this baby be mine?

When the Chinese don't understand a request for an extra-large T-shirt, a box for shipping, or a bottle of water, they say vehemently, "Don't have!" even if the object you're asking for is in plain sight. It's a good all-purpose answer—better to save face than to admit they don't understand.

I rock and sway until Sophie's head hangs forward and her eyes drop shut, followed by the dreaded but inevitable moment when she jerks back to consciousness, shrieking at me as if I've tricked her, betrayed her, lost her trust for lulling her toward sleep.

What does she want? What am I supposed to do? I don't know, don't understand.

"Don't have," I want to say. "No, no, don't have."

Every day, Sophie has slept a little more than the day before, but still not enough: sleep only exists for her as a battle she loses, and as soon as she replenishes the bare minimum of necessary fuel, she's primed for fighting again.

Maybe she's still grieving, maybe she's still not sure of me, maybe it's not the antihistamines. Sleeping in the presence of another requires enormous trust, a willingness to temporarily relinquish whatever hold you think you have on your world. How does an abandoned child allow herself to be subconscious and completely vulnerable?

Jody wants to go to the Night Market.

"Me too," I say.

"No one is taking babies with them," Jody says. And she grumbles, something about starting to feel like my slave.

I back off. Of course she should be the one to go.

I walk Sophie up and down the hall, suppressing my fierce urge to beg Jody to stay, not leave me alone with my baby. I'm panicked at the full knowledge that this baby is mine. Mine alone. My responsibility alone. I'm her mom forever and ever.

Other people can sleep and read books cover to cover and think straight long enough to do long division in their heads. Other people can take off for the beach on the spur of the moment or run down the street to the drugstore or go out to the market at night. These things are over for me. I will watch hours, days, years go by, cooped up with this fussy baby. How am I going to manage alone with her in South Carolina?

At seven, Jody has forgotten about the market, and when I remind her, she responds lackadaisically.

I teeter on the precipice of indecision, conscience warring with desire. Would it be so wrong to talk Jody into staying this once, or would I merely be giving in to my frantic need to hold despair at bay?

I push Jody out the door because I have to face down my fear sometime. As soon as she's gone, I collapse into a chair and cry.

Maybe some people—the other single women in my travel group, Jody, some of my friends who are good with babies—maybe they are so cut out to be parents, it doesn't matter if they're single or married. Not me. I have kidded myself. I will never be able to do this alone.

I remember the studies on sleep deprivation I read about in psych classes. I understood intellectually the case histories and statistics. I aced the tests. But this is the first time I've really understood how the loss of deep sleep and dreams can deprive a person of brightness and hope.

I fix a bottle and feed Sophie. Rare peace steals over her face as she focuses all her energy on sucking down formula. I concentrate on her face to filter out all the things that feel unbearable: the screams that still echo in my ringing ears, the endless hum of traffic and bleating of horns outside, the thick, sticky, steamy, sun-beaten heat whenever I step out the door, my insatiable thirst, no ice, walking, walking, walking, sore throat, sore back, not enough food, not enough sleep, the pitying glances of other parents, agency employees who stroll empty-handed and offer no help, ancestors who made the decision for all of us to stand upright without thinking through the consequences. Irrational resentment, numbing fatigue, unpredictable waves of panic and despair.

It's an effort to haul myself to my feet. Change Sophie into a nightgown. Lay her on the bed surrounded by her toys.

She sings to herself and jabbers and tests the sounds of round rattle against small stacking cup, long rattle against medium stacking cup, big stacking cups against little stacking cups. Whatever subtle variations in tone keep her going, I don't hear them. It's all noise to me. But she's happily occupied, and there's no way I'm going to interfere.

I order room service, wash bottles, mix formula for the night, sort laundry, and lay out shirts, pants, and socks for tomorrow.

I'm so, so tired of washing out bottles in hotel rooms and wearing the same clothes over and over and mixing formula and rice cereal in the bathroom sink and sleeping as if aligned on railroad tracks, muscles braced for the slightest vibration, ears always attuned for the oncoming train.

Alone in this room I can no longer avoid the questions I've been afraid to ask: What if Sophie's incessant agitation is not, after all, a symptom of drugs or grief?

What if this is her temperament?

And what if I just can't handle it?

Yet already, each morning when I first see her, it's as if I've known her forever, as if she's always belonged to me. What am I going to do?

This is the real trap of parenthood, the thing that no one warned me about. I'm not stuck. I could catch the next flight out of here. I could give her back to the orphanage. I could let Jody adopt her.

But these aren't really options, because even while my teeth are chomping at the bars of my cage, even as my hands itch to release the lock and my feet lift in preparation to run, my heart refuses to participate in any escape plans.

This baby is mine, and I'm hers, and there's no turning back.

I don't know whether to be upset or relieved at this revelation. So instead I wander over to check on her.

Her chest rises and falls, her eyelashes fluttering against her cheek.

She's asleep.

Asleep, without any effort from me.

I hardly know what to do with myself. The possibilities, magnificently liberating, unreel before me. I could read a whole page without interruption, write a coherent paragraph in my journal, take a shower, turn on the TV for the first time and listen to people speaking in Chinese.

But first I remove the silver lid from my dinner, now cold. I unfold the white napkin and dish rice onto a plate. Ping Ping used to make fun of me for eating fried rice. She said that the Chinese people only eat their rice fried to disguise days-old leftovers. But now this cold food smells heavenly.

I'm sitting in a hotel room while the sky darkens outside, scooping up bites from a serving dish on a low desk, propping my plate on my knees, taking big bites of pork and eggs and rice, feeling like I'm at a banquet. For once, I eat and eat, and cry grateful tears.

The next morning I announce that I'm taking Sophie off the antihistamines, against Shiyan's instructions.

In fact, I'm feeling really defiant. I dress Sophie in shorts.

"Shiyan's going to have a fit," Jody says.

"Yeah," I answer.

We smile at each other.

It could be a self-fulfilling prophecy, or it could be that Sophie's getting used to me or simply feeling better, or it could be that for once she slept a whole night. Whatever the cause, she settles down considerably. She continues to exhibit powerful emotions that shift with no notice, and she still resists sleep a little. But the upward swing in all of our moods is palpable.

Over the next few months, back in the United States, her pediatrician will prescribe a variety of antihistamines, and each time they will wire her. She will chant and yell all night, fierce and noisy. Doubting my judgment, I will give her milk once more, and the diarrhea and rash will immediately return.

We would never have made it without Jody; without her gentle skill with Sophie, without all of her behind-the-scenes work that kept our room organized and our clothes washed and Sophie fed, the tasks in front of me would have felt insurmountable.

But I can't get over the fact that I, so clearly not a natural with babies, so clearly confused and lost and overwhelmed, I, *I* was right. Sophie needed me too. How quickly I knew for sure that she was mine, lactose intolerant like me, adverse to antihistamines like me, intense, sensitive, moody: my child.

One night, a bunch of dads take a taxi to McDonald's and bring back hamburgers and pepper burgers. We spread out bags and paper wrappers in the hall, which soon fills with the greasy, salty smell of American french fries.

The babies are coming alive. Sick Bridget's perpetual worry lines iron smooth. Long-legged Lily smiles more than she trembles. Rebecca's tin-kling little laugh rings out, now a familiar sound. Scrappy Gina kicks like mad and grabs everyone's water bottles. Tiny, quiet Victoria babbles non-stop.

Sophie's hand ranges around after hamburger wrappers, fries, Gina's legos, my discarded pickle. I slide and shove things out of her way. Non-plussed, she keeps reaching, stretching, straining. And I'm struck by how lively she is, how beautiful, how perfect.

See, she's not always noisy and fussy, I want to tell the group. I want to nudge Jody, point out that we really did get the best one.

Up and down the hall, parents and helpers bend adoring faces toward their children, and in everyone's eyes there is wonder, there is smugness, there is the secret thought restrained only by politeness—that every one of us is sure that we got the best one.

4

The next Saturday, we learn that NATO, in its Yugoslavian war, has bombed the Chinese embassy in Belgrade, killing three and injuring twenty. The United States claims that the bombing was an unfortunate accident due to a lack of comprehensive and accurate maps. The Chinese news calls it a wanton and barbarous act.

We only learn of this because of Jody's lifelong tendency to snap on the TV during lulls, a habit that has always annoyed me. We watch a tape of people marching outside the U.S. embassy in Beijing, shouting, "Down with American imperialism" and throwing bricks.

I question Shiyan. She refuses to discuss the news. It feels as if she is withholding information out of some notion of protecting us.

I don't want to be protected. I am restless with curiosity.

Deep down, I don't really believe that we are in any danger. We're far from the demonstrations, and I possess papers in two languages confirming that this baby is mine. Besides, I don't want to be overdramatic, a cardinal sin in my family when I was growing up. When I complained about persistent headaches, my mom said, "Maybe you have a brain tumor" and snorted with laughter. I secretly lay awake at night, worrying that I was dying of a brain tumor, but I was terrified to ask the doctor about it lest he erupt into manic laughter, too. One time I passed out from heat exhaustion, and my mom dismissed it on the phone to a friend: "She must have seen a bug or something." My mother's lack of concern both offended me and proved oddly calming. My dad rolled his eyes as if I were the drama queen of all time when, at thirteen, I wanted to back out of a birthday party because my card was bigger than my present . . . okay, I'll give him that one.

As an adult, I fear being thought too emotional, irrational, flaky, unprofessional, or weak, so I convert sadness to anger as quickly as possible to preserve my dignity, carefully contain pleasure lest it be seen as arrogance or foolishness, and downplay fear or anxiety so as not to seem overdramatic. Facing the backlash to the bombing, and based on no logic but the flawed assumption that historical moments happen to people in history texts and novels, not us, I conclude—luckily with some accuracy—that there is no reason for us to be nervous.

I doubt that this senseless loss of life protested all over China will be more than a sound byte on the news at home. After all, my parents still don't call or e-mail. If we appeared to be in danger, surely they would express some alarm.

If I weren't in a sleep-deprived haze, conserving every ounce of energy to keep my baby fed and changed and washed and calm, I might feel more than a twinge of hurt, irritation, or concern at my parents' seeming lack of interest. As it is, I register it as a flicker of resentment at how turmoil in my life barely translates into blips on my parents' radar, but I don't dwell on it. Jody calls her parents to reassure them that we are all right. I don't call mine. I imagine them on the other end, puzzled that I'm spending so much money to call them from China. I can hear them wondering: Why wouldn't I be all right?

While we wait to leave Hangzhou to go on to the U.S. consulate for our daughters' visas, the adoptive families in Guangzhou, our destination, are temporary prisoners in their hotels. According to the state-run Xinhua news agency, tens of thousands of students have arrived in buses and converged on the U.S., French, Italian, and Dutch consulates. The only words the adoptive families can make out are "American killers. American killers. American killers." The new parents are warned by hotel staff to stay away from windows; hotel security and military police have been stationed beside outside doors. The Americans remain bewildered about what's going on until they catch CNN reports of Chinese protestors attacking the U.S. embassy in Beijing and setting fire to a building in the U.S. consulate compound in Chengdu.

Demonstrations in Guangzhou are described as well orchestrated. Neatly dressed students carry professionally made signs as they chant and burn American flags. One news agency estimates the "shouting mobs" surrounding the embassies and western hotels at more than ten thousand. An American woman first glimpses the crowds swelling around the White Swan Hotel and assumes that they are marking some Chinese holiday. "There's a big parade!" she shouts to her husband.

In fact, as Jeanette Chu of the INS Adoption Unit explains in an e-mail to adoptive parents, this is an especially sensitive time with two imminent anniversaries: the tenth one of the Tiananmen Square "incident" in June, which the American press typically calls not an "incident" but a "massacre," and the fiftieth anniversary of the founding of the Chinese government in October. Perhaps those upcoming dates add to the volatility of reactions. At any rate, the U.S. Department of State sends an urgent message asking U.S. citizens in the PRC to "review their security practices, maintain a low profile, stay alert to the changing situation, and avoid demonstrations."

We don't find out any of this till much later. Despite the fact that she speaks Chinese and could choose to update us, Shiyan remains close-mouthed. Oblivious to the seriousness of the situation, I simply decide not to dress Sophie in the red, white, and blue outfit I was saving for her consulate appointment.

Sunday is Mother's Day. At breakfast, Pam's sister Connie brings Pam a carnation. An anti-American demonstration passes our hotel. Chinese customers in the restaurant clap and cheer.

It's raining. Late in the morning while Sophie drops asleep to Jody's sway and hum, I gaze out of our seventeenth-floor room at skyscrapers topped with Chinese billboards and towering over squat, dilapidated apartment buildings. Most of the windows are slanted open, lines of laundry wet in the rain.

Sophie has been sleeping a lot since we abandoned her medication. Even when she's asleep, I hear the sound of her cry in my head. Even when she's in her crib, the memory of her weight remains in my arms. I feel weepy at least five times a day, equally moved by kind gestures, TV commercials in Chinese, angry fist waving by demonstrators on the news, and the repeated realization that I am now a mother. And now, while I watch

Sophie sleep, all I can think is that the people killed in the NATO bombing were each somebody's child.

After lunch at another restaurant piping in Christmas carols and "Auld Lang Syne," Shiyan offers to take us to the foreign language bookstore. I hate to pass up the opportunity to be near books. Jody takes Sophie back to the hotel.

Bookstores and office supply stores are places where I feel completely happy. I can wander for hours among shelves of books, stacks of paper, and displays of pens, folders, and staplers. I don't quite understand why people decorate their homes and offices with paintings, posters, and knickknacks when a wall of books and a jar of pens is so much more interesting, so beautiful, so rich with possibility.

So even though almost all of the books in this store are in Chinese, I feel at home for the first time in weeks. I wander up and down aisles, past a big *Titanic* poster, randomly pulling out books and shuffling through their tissue-thin pages, wishing I could read the spidery characters.

I happen across some English anthologies of translated short stories and compilations of Chinese sayings, and I stop to examine covers and bindings and read a few paragraphs here and there. I flip through some stories by Ding Ling and wonder if the store has a translation of her book *Miss Sophie's Diary*. Back when I chose my daughter's name, I didn't know that Sophie was the title character in a short story collection by a prominent twentieth-century Chinese writer.

Shiyan leans against a wall, looking bored. She has offered to help us find whatever we're looking for, so I approach her. "I'm looking for a book by Ding Ling," I say.

"Who?" she asks in a too-loud voice, familiar scorn curling her lip.

"Ding Ling, the writer," I say, although what I really want to do is mutter "Forget it" and shrink away, maybe crawl under the floor tiles and make myself a little permanent nest there away from the light of day.

"Who?" She raises her voice so that even non-English-speakers can't miss her contempt. Suddenly I notice how hot the store is. My cheeks burn. I must have it wrong. There is no writer named Ding Ling. What kind of name is that, anyway? And why would a Chinese writer call her book *Miss Sophie's Diary*?

Then I recover my senses. Shiyan is not going to succeed at intimidating me. Books are my turf, even if everything in sight is in Chinese.

"Ding Ling," I repeat. I can play the intimidation game, too. "The twentieth-century writer," I say, in my best crisp professorial voice, copying Shiyan's characteristic impatient tone.

We glare at each other while around us customers poke through bins of books and "Doe a deer" plays on the sound system.

"I'll go ask." Shiyan backs down. Uncertainty flickers across her face before she adjusts her expression back to its usual disdain. But for just a second I have glimpsed, beneath her brusque, haughty manner, the insecure human being who is as terrified as I am of being thought stupid.

I will never grow to like Shiyan, but the knowledge that secretly she's afraid of the same thing I am will get me through the rest of the trip. All along she's been afraid that I'll be the one to find her out, and now I have.

"They don't have it," she yells to me. I could swear there's a triumphant gleam in her eye. I may know something about books and writers, but I am in her power: I can neither read nor speak Chinese, and must take her word for it.

Back at the hotel, Sophie's asleep again. Jody repeats a news bulletin: U.S. embassies in China will be closed Monday and Tuesday.

Our embassy appointment is Tuesday. I ask Shiyan about it when several of us meet in her room to go over INS paperwork.

Shiyan shrugs, annoyance flickering across her face. I get the feeling she wants to confiscate our TV. There's nothing to worry about, she says, but doesn't elaborate.

We turn our attention to the forms we'll need. I've organized my documents and copies according to instructions from the agency. Shiyan directs us to remove all but a few papers.

I've been carrying my baby's weight in papers. So far, we have only turned over a single page—our visa pictures. It's dawning on me that we aren't going to need most of these documents at all.

Shiyan tells us not to bother to read the pages of questions. Just check no for each one, she says. I rebel and read them anyway. Each time we check "no" we are testifying that our children have not worked as spies, have not smuggled for another government, and have not been prostitutes, pimps, or agents of destruction.

Tense, tired, and punchy, we giggle a lot over our own lame jokes. Shiyan has probably heard it all before. She doesn't crack a smile.

Herb and Joe head off for their nightly McDonald's run. They come back, shaken. The restaurant is dark and deserted, with a sign: Closed until Further Notice.

All the American businesses are closed.

After this sinks in, Connie says she doesn't think we should go to the night market. Others agree nervously. Maybe Americans shouldn't be running around outside right now.

Brandy and I scoff. We are going.

We have no idea that mobs in Guangzhou surrounded the White Swan Hotel and the embassies last night, that it took sixty Chinese officers to hold them back from storming the hotel's lobby. Police formed lines in front of the embassies, pushing back those who tried to break in. In Beijing, protestors threw eggs, potatoes, and stones at the U.S. embassy, shattering windows.

Later I will discover that Jeanette Chu has sent out a notice to families en route to Guangzhou, telling them to avoid hotels near the foreign consulates. "If you're not already at the White Swan, PLEASE STAY PUT," she writes.

Back at home, my colleagues watch the news and wonder where I am. Caroline and the dean call my parents. My dad answers. He's been ill. When the dean identifies himself and the college, Dad says, confused, "Well, now, that sounds familiar" before he figures out that it's my workplace. A couple from Washington who adopted from the same orphanage track Caroline down by e-mail; they are part of an effort to locate adoptive parents in China and make sure that we get processed. Caroline has no idea where I am.

On Sunday, Jeanette Chu sends out an update: "The situation in China remains highly volatile but also variable by location." The White Swan, she reports, "remains 'business as usual,' and several families were enjoying the barbecue buffet this evening."

While families at the White Swan Hotel enjoy the barbecue buffet, Herb, Connie, Brandy, and I head through dark streets to the night market. It feels strange and illicit to be outside after dark, past my new bedtime. It feels weird not to be carrying a baby. When I turn my head or shake it, I picture the way Sophie whips her head around when she's startled and thrashes it when she's tired. I am taking on her mannerisms. I am becoming my child.

It's so odd, so wonderful, to be an autonomous person with arms hanging loose, light and moving freely, alert to stars and lights and the wafting smell of dumplings, the rise and fall of voices, the textures of silk and enamel and jade. I can mosey down rows of wood-plank tables, poking through heaps of scarves, rows of vases, teapots, and harmony balls, hanging bars of silk robes, piles of jade rings and pendants. Mao kitsch fills whole tables: little red books, buttons, lighters, T-shirts, statues. Connie bargains for my few small souvenirs—a scarf, a wall-hanging of zodiac animals, a set of harmony balls, and a bag for carrying my documents to Guangzhou. I breathe in warm, humid air, shake my head at vendors who thrust small, tacky objects at me, and wish to walk forever.

But whenever I hear a baby cry, I start, shift into a mild panic: what did I do with Sophie? It takes a second for my head to clear each time, for me to remember that she's back at the hotel. I wonder if I will ever again be able to go anywhere without her and not feel that something's missing. Our expedition to the night market is uneventful, as I expected, but even if there were any danger, I'd be in denial. I am not willing to imagine any obstacles that could keep me from leaving China with my baby.

In the morning we catch our plane to Guangzhou. The social workers drop casual comments about the demonstrations, then go silent, looking guilty, like they've been instructed not to reveal what they know. I'm getting antsy. I hate not knowing what's going on.

We head to the White Swan in a bus with drawn curtains. Buses pass us, filled with students returning home after carrying signs all day. We inch forward, stop, creep a few more feet, stop. Through gaps in the curtains we can see people marching and chanting and hoisting banners while crowds swarm around. *No more murders,* says one of the few signs in English. *Accident true lie. Stop bombing. A tooth for a tooth. Give me justice. Blood for blood. Condolences to the Dead.*

Shiyan's skill and calm reveal themselves in her quiet maneuvering. As much as she irritates me, I have to admire the way that, efficiently and without fanfare, she gets us to where we need to be. First we stop at a small photo shop for the babies' visa pictures. Then she sneaks us through the White Swan's back doors. There, she gives us instructions: Avoid the demonstrators in front of the building. Do not leave under any circumstances. All tours in Guangzhou have been cancelled.

Finally, a chance to rest and ease Sophie into a routine. Still, my curiosity is driving me crazy. I mix with some pale tourists speaking German and edge over to the doors, briefly observing a line of protestors shuffling along, placards swaying low in tired arms.

In our room, I plunk Sophie into the crib, which has rows of beads along either side, like abacuses. I show her how if she lies down she can play with the beads on both sides. She thinks this is really cool. She chortles and bangs the beads until she falls asleep.

"Smarter than your average bear," Jody says approvingly, and once again I'm amazed that I know how to be a mom.

At dinner, I skim the *China Daily*. The language has been carefully chosen to provoke outrage at the U.S. government. Journalism standards are clearly different here, this reporting overtly political compared to the more subtle biases of the "objective" American press. But the fact remains that someone's children died because of my government's carelessness.

Sophie fusses all night. After a bottle and diaper change at five-thirty, I give up on sleep. Sophie stares up at me from her crib, saying "Mamamamamama," and Jody and I laugh at how I can't hold anything against her.

She drops off again at six. I send Jody down to breakfast without us. I pick up the room, make formula, fix myself some oatmeal, and gaze out at the river, misty in the morning fog, crawling with barges that steadily blast their horns. This is pretty much all I'll see of Guangzhou.

I page through the *China Daily*. One man's body is described as "painfully distorted," his wife's hardly recognizable. Only fifteen minutes before the bombing started, the newspaper reports, the wife had mentioned "her plan to have a baby during their vacation this year."

"I quivered when I learnt they were bloodily murdered," says a "sorrow-stricken" friend.

The sister-in-law of another dead journalist says that her husband smashed the family's TV set to prevent his elderly parents from viewing the news.

"We gave them tranquilizers before telling them the truth, but they were too grief-stricken to take the sudden loss of their daughter," the sister-in-law says.

These details are designed to provoke tears and outrage, and combined with new-mom hormones and wretched exhaustion, I'm a sobbing mess in no time. As I watch Sophie sleeping and imagine her birth mother walking away from her, I'm overtaken by fresh torrents of grief: how could anyone turn her back on my baby?

It is a terrible reality I will always struggle with, a shock to the system. That Sophie belonged to someone else before she belonged to me. That that other woman, that first mother, made a desperate choice I cannot imagine as anything but the beginning of a permanent hole in her heart. Sitting there while barges coast by outside, I'm sad for this woman and angry with her and grateful to her all at once, and sadder still because life is so fickle that with a shift of circumstances I could be her, someone enduring the exact same terrible loss.

I try to get a grip, but I am really, really tired.

Our group meets at the elevator at seven-fifty. A new dad from another agency says that when he went out with his baby, demonstrators yelled at him to go home. We descend with trepidation and take taxis a few blocks. The morning is quiet and warm, and as we weave through back streets we see no demonstrators, only white-haired people doing Tai Chi in the park.

The taxi lets us off at a corner. We walk a couple of blocks on uneven sidewalk tiles to the clinic.

There, I am too busy juggling the diaper bag, Sophie, our passports, and the forms to note our surroundings or her measurements. Three doctors see her in rapid succession. They listen to her heart, weigh her, and peer into her eyes and ears and throat. She cries and watches me fearfully, waiting for me to save her.

When we arrive back at our room, it's still a mess—wet towels wadded across the bathroom floor, beds unmade, laundry hunching in big plastic bags near the door, waiting to be picked up. We smooth out one of the beds in preparation for the visa interview. Ever since Secretary of State Madeleine Albright intervened, consulate officials have been conducting visa interviews at the White Swan.

Our interviewer finishes with a family down the hall and knocks on our door at ten. I gather documents, $325 in the U.S. money I've almost forgotten how to count, visa photos, and the sealed medical records delivered only minutes before by John, our Guangzhou translator. I hand over my INS forms and tax returns, barely daring to breathe. Ordinarily, I've heard, consulate officials and assistants review these thoroughly. Often adoptive parents have to fax home for further documentation.

I've been worried about this, since I have no official tax returns or records. I've telefiled the last three years; my only documentation is worksheets complete with doodling and to-do lists in the margins. I tried to get printouts from the IRS before I left, but that was around April 15, and they were a little preoccupied. I've been braced this whole trip to face a paper-work nightmare when it came time to get Sophie's visa.

So I'm a little tense as we perch on unmade beds to start the interview. I apologize for the state of our room, but the official reassures me that she's used to it. She's been speed-processing families for the last two days; thir-ty came here yesterday from other hotels. Ours will be an abbreviated ver-sion of normal procedures—unlike usually, there will be no time and no assistant for combing through the paperwork.

I fight a big, relieved, goofy, ear-to-ear smile and keep my tone level so as not to betray my joy at this news. The woman asks a couple of ques-tions, I swear that everything in my paperwork is true, and that is that.

We join other parents and babies camping out on blankets at the end of the hall. The hotel seems populated entirely by American parents with their Chinese girls. Sophie looks round and plump and sturdy next to the other emaciated babies. A set of twins her age are half her size.

"*That's* a healthy one," a passerby remarks. Later, I will be surprised that Sophie is in the lower percentiles of the American growth charts: I have be-come accustomed to thinking of her as chubby, teetering toward obesity.

From Brandy's window, I see that the demonstrations are thinning, the marching and chanting ebbing. The crowd straggling along outside is sub-dued.

As soon as our room has been cleaned, I send out our laundry and head downstairs to a mall selling beautiful hand-carved wooden trunks, diapers and wipes, and American junk food. I spend my last yuan on Chinese chil-dren's books.

Back upstairs, Jody tells me that the agency has changed our plane tick-ets. We're leaving in two hours. We wolf down box lunches, retrieve our dirty laundry, and hurry to pack and pile our suitcases in the hall. I pre-pare formula, change money, check out. Home! No more hours cooped up in a hotel. No more living out of suitcases. We are going home.

Pam and Lily pass in the hall, Lily wobbling on her long legs while Pam holds her hands like a puppeteer.

"She can only walk without her pants," Pam calls.

We wait and wait. Finally, the visas arrive, and we're off to Hong Kong.

All I feared about parenthood has come true in spectacular ways dur-ing our stay in China. That I would be too absorbed in the mechanics of daily living to absorb the details, to attend fully to bombs dropping and people dying. That I would be confined, restless, too busy navigating each hour to participate in the greater adventures around me. My world has narrowed, and if I had time, I might lament this.

But the trip home is grueling, grueling work, briskly crossing airports tugging a diaper bag, a carry-on, and a sixteen-pound baby, waiting in the endlessly snaking lines for Immigration, passing through X-ray machines, showing documents. Sophie snatches her visa and wads it up. I still her hands right before they close around her passport. I'm alert for places to sit, even for a few seconds or a minute or two. My ears ring from airplane noise and buzz with exhaustion, and my feet and back ache by the time we arrive at our Hong Kong airport hotel, a Futurama area complete with eerie space-age music and a stage like a flying saucer in the middle of the lobby. We are so worn out and disoriented we might as well be on another planet.

Up at five, we walk what seems the entire length of the Hong Kong airport to change tickets, our babies fascinated by their reflections in the marble countertops. We negotiate too-big luggage carts between plastic McDonald's seats, wait for hours, crowd forward to board. In Tokyo we observe the gradual transition to westernization in the higher cotton content of the clothes and the alternating toilet stalls, the familiar western seats mixed in with Chinese squat versions.

On the long, long flight to Detroit, turbulence rocks Sophie to sleep. She stretches out on my lap, tosses around trying to get comfortable, wakes, sleeps again, wakes again in a fury of discomfort. My sneeze startles her. She screams as if it were a gunshot. She refuses to eat and her cheeks are feverish. Tired as she is, our surroundings are so interesting that all she wants to do is hang by her toes from our seat, twisting around to play with a Japanese child behind us. I contort my arms to keep her from falling on her head.

I can't sleep, can't reach my headphones or reading glasses. Sophie drinks formula and promptly spits up on me. Fatigue makes me limp. My skin feels bruised after hours of friction with Sophie's skin and clothing. I keep trying to pass her to Jody. Each time, Sophie sends up a heartbreaking wail.

My arms will give way if I try to hold her any longer. When I relinquish her, she hollers and hollers, her voice hoarse and ragged. Her hands flail, trying to find me, clutch at me, hold me in place. I drop fast through time and space.

Sorry, baby, I think.

Sophie's fist gropes out blindly, closes around a handful of my shirt.

Gripping me, she, too, sleeps.

Detroit, 2:30 P.M., except to us it's 2:30 A.M. and the daylight and the bright lights and the bustling rested people whose luggage wheels clamor efficiently along the tiles are like profanities. We wait in a motionless line for Immigration. Move, stop, move, stop, hand over Sophie's mangled visa packet. An official stamps her passport and issues a temporary green card authorizing her for employment.

We've lost most of our group. We hug Pam, Connie, Brandy, and Brandy's parents goodbye. Lily and Gina are scrubbed and chipper in clean, frilly dresses, hair ribbons, white socks, and new shoes, all ready to greet their families and the press in Detroit.

Jody and I haul our stuff through customs.

"Welcome to the U.S.A.," an official says to Sophie, ticking her under the chin. A moment that should be full of fanfare, balloons and streamers and confetti.

Sophie's cheeks blaze. At our gate, I beg for an empty seat for my sick baby. The airline obliges.

By the time we land in Kansas City, my clothes are stiff with dried spit up, hair limp, skin grimy. Seat lint coats Sophie's clothes. Her hair is soaking wet and her socks no longer white but gray, a bewildering development in someone who can't walk. Her face is as red as that of an angry man on the verge of a heart attack, an actress who uses stage makeup designed to be seen from the back of the theater. A new tooth gleams in her lower gum.

Even if I'd packed a homecoming outfit for Sophie or a change of clothes for me, I wouldn't have the energy to clean us up. My one gesture at celebration, the little sticky wings from the airline, promptly fall off Sophie's T-shirt.

Though most members of our group are met at their final destinations by local press and though several families arriving in Kansas City that week are on the news, our welcoming party is mercifully small—my parents, aunt, uncle, and some cousins.

I blink at my dad's video camera and pat Sophie's back reassuringly. Am I relieved to be home? Excited to be a mom? Have Sophie and I bonded? I give the expected answers.

The truth is that I've lost the capacity to experience distinct emotions. They're all tumbled together like clothes in a washer, sodden, misshapen garments that I will later pluck out one by one, disentangling relief from anxiety, joy from despair, love from indifference. I will slowly try on once-familiar emotions like clothes I temporarily forgot I owned, gradually reinhabiting them.

For now, adrenaline keeps me going. But all of my daydreams are about sleeping long and soundly, a deep restful slumber filled with dreams I'll remember when I finally wake.

Missouri

5

Jet lag for adults is a breeze compared to the bewilderment of a baby with no internalized conventions that make her long to sleep when it's dark and stay alert in the light.

At Jody's house, Sophie and I go to bed at eleven. I shed my filthy clothes and leave them puddled on the floor. I shed consciousness just as quickly.

Three hours later, Sophie cries.

I come to, yanked abruptly from silky far-away deep-down sleep. This has to be the bleakest moment I have ever known. I stumble from bed through the pitch dark.

I lift Sophie out of her crib. Tears of pure exhaustion race each other down my face.

My parents are asleep in the next room. Jody has vacated the house for us and gone to sleep at her parents'. So far, my mom, though delighted by her new granddaughter, seems frenzied and anxious with her. And Dad is unusually tired and spacey.

There is no tension, just the usual denial that misunderstandings could ever exist and the general goodwill that mark the beginnings of all our interactions, as if each new meeting is a clean slate and this time we will get it right. Clearly, my dad's recent illness accounts for their silence while I was in China.

I wish they would get up and offer to take Sophie so I can sleep, but I don't hear any stirring from their room. I sit on the living room floor while Sophie talks and sings and bangs her stacking cups and rattles.

I'm immobile, despairing, remembering how people in sleep deprivation experiments become so deranged it seems perfectly rational and desirable to jump off of tall buildings or throw themselves in front of trains.

At four o'clock, Sophie drops off again. Gently, I settle her in the portacrib and slide between my sheets, sleeping and listening at the same time. Sophie snores, then goes quiet. I leap out of bed to make sure she's still breathing.

When I close my eyes her face is imprinted on the inside of my eyelids, mouth scrunched up. The memory of her cry plays inside my head. I sleep and float back toward consciousness, my arms surprised not to be holding her. Where is she? Is that the baby heaped on the end of my bed? I sit up, horrified, then realize the lump is the blankets I have tossed back.

Finally, I black out. At five-thirty, she howls again. For another hour she plays on the living room floor while I lie on the rug. My hope fountains up whenever she rubs her eyes or tugs at her hair.

Please, please help me, I want to call out to my sleeping parents. Please do something.

My parents are almost seventy years old. They need their sleep, and besides, Sophie has fits if anyone but me tries to hold her. My parents' eagerness for her to take to them, their anxiety that she won't, charges the air, makes everyone nervous. It would be pointless for me to wake them.

I think of that saying about the darkest hour being before the dawn. Dawn seems ages away. I lie on the floor wondering if it can possibly get any darker.

Sophie goes to sleep at six-thirty. Back to bed for another two and a half hours. At nine we get up. By noon we're both asleep again, me with a pounding headache, feeling like a train's been barreling over me all night.

At the Shipleys' for dinner, Sophie willingly goes to my tall male cousins who adore babies. They know just how to hold her and talk to her. If it wouldn't hurt my parents' feelings, I would beg my cousins to come stay at Jody's, too.

I haven't been alone for three weeks. I fantasize about being in my own house, where I will rock Sophie in the La-Z-Boy, read while she plays, write during naps, and wash bottles in the dishwasher. My ordinary life sounds foreign and luxurious.

But in South Carolina, I'll be on my own. How will I eat and sleep, shower and run errands? Sophie still wails when confined in high chairs. I gave up on the frontpack carrier back in Hangzhou, where I bought an umbrella stroller that she wouldn't sit in. I left that behind in Hong Kong. Sophie screamed all the way from the airport in the car seat so that conversation was impossible. She howls when left in a crib and protested at the top of her lungs throughout the one bath Jody and I gave her.

How am I going to manage even the simplest task? How will I ever take care of her alone?

At ten-thirty in the evening, Sophie is up again. We've slept less than an hour. There is no sound from behind my parents' closed door.

Bright-eyed and energetic, Sophie plays contentedly. Resigned, I write in my journal and then doze on the living room rug.

At three o'clock she konks out on the floor. Elation surges through me. With trembling joy I anticipate sleep. Sleep! I waste five minutes rhapsodizing about sleep as I get comfortable in my bed. I have come to feel about sleep the way I used to about an upcoming date with someone I was head over heels in love with. Sleep: I settle happily into it and dream about it. I dream I am sleeping. I dream that I dream that I am sleeping. I descend down through layer after layer of sleep, silk and cotton and soft, soft feathers.

At three-fifteen, Sophie cries.

I reenter the world shocked, wondering if this is how it feels to be born, one minute immersed in warm amniotic fluids, the next shot into glaring lights and batteringly loud noises.

Sophie has evidently made a resolution never to sleep again. She sits on the floor or flips onto her back, bonking herself on the head with rattles and cups, the whole familiar routine, yanking at her hair, yelling and screeching and thrashing and forcing her drooping eyes back open as she howls with rage at that enemy stalking her, sleep.

At seven, my mother has the ill luck to pass through on her way to the bathroom. Next thing she knows, she's holding a baby and I'm back in bed. When Sophie catches on that I've left her, she unleashes a torrent of angry screams.

In my sleep I hear her fussing, and Mom jostling her and singing "Rock a Bye Baby" in a scratchy voice and at a frenzied tempo, then segueing into a game of "This Little Piggy Went to Market" recited so fast and frantically, I know I should intervene before Mom dislocates my baby's toes. But I can't move, can't wake fully. In my dreams I am consumed by guilt, as if I have abandoned her. My poor baby has already been given away twice in her short life; now I've left her, too.

I wake with tears in my eyes and then I go right back to sleep.

Of course she wants to sleep all day, but I wake her after less than four hours in the hope that she'll sleep tonight. And she does: for two hours. Then I'm weaving out of bed to the kitchen where I turn on the country music station that has started to sedate her in the car seat. I sink onto the couch. In my lap, Sophie gives me an adoring look and makes a kissy mouth.

I think of all my friends who say that parenthood has made them more compassionate, centered, and creative. Now I understand that they are mistaking passivity borne of exhaustion for kindness and sleep-deprived hallucinations for creativity. My world feels as narrow as the strips of darkness outside the blinds. My center floats away like blurred far-off headlights.

I travel through the same emotional loop every few hours, the same stunning revelations: bouts of bottomless despair, a recurring bleak, stunned recognition of what my life has become, the startling realization that even if some rich, stable, experienced person offered to take this baby off my hands, I've never reached a point even close to saying yes.

I'm constantly surprised at myself. I think of all the pets I've been through, all the friends and lovers I've had to let go of. Separation was never painless, but I moved on. My guinea pigs, cats, ex-husband, and childhood best friend didn't launch constant assaults on my eardrums or refuse to let me sleep, didn't demand all of my attention or expect me to fill their gaping, endless needs. They never left me so tired I thought I would keel over dead at any minute. So why has life without this baby become the one unthinkable thought?

I swear that Sophie was a cat in another life. Jody's moody white cat Agatha prowls under living room chairs and slinks down the stairs, never taking her eyes off the noisy creature who has taken over her house. Sophie growls at her toys, she cries with the rise and fall of a cat in heat, she roars in a tiger-hoarse voice when she's sleepy, she claws at me with her little fingernails, and when she's congested and content, her breathing sounds like a purr.

Twelve-thirty in the morning. I've fed Sophie a bottle, changed her diaper, and spent an hour laying out clothes and packing the diaper bag for the gathering at my aunt's house later. Sophie's on the floor kicking, talking, and avoiding sleep at all costs. If I even close my eyes, she whimpers.

Why did I ever think I cared about the classic philosophical questions, whether the chicken or egg came first, whether genes or environment are more influential, whether a tree falling in a forest where there's no one to hear makes a sound, whether God can create a stone so heavy that even he can't lift it?

All I want to know is, will this baby ever sleep? Will I ever sleep again?

Country music softly plays while I rock from foot to foot. The silhouette of branches and leaves nod in a breeze. There's some song about how God spent more time on you than on other people, followed by one about a river that isn't really a river but a metaphor for life's journey.

I used to be cynical. I thought these songs were trite, dopey, chock-full of whining, sentimentality, and unhealthy relationships. But my God, I've never really listened. They are about my baby. They are beautiful tender tributes to children. All of my life, how have I failed to see this?

I stand swaying in Jody's kitchen in the middle of the night, moved and overwhelmed at how our lives follow the current, dump us into the shallows, pick us up and sweep us on. This is life with a baby. This is profound.

God, I'm tired.

And then the stacking cups Sophie clutches in each fist clatter to the floor, one, then the other. She's asleep.

Fifteen minutes later: indignant yell from the crib. You'd think I'd come to expect this, quit feeling such keen disappointment every time.

We walk, we talk, we play, I let her cry, I plug her mouth with a pacifier and surprise her into temporary silence, I lie beside her on the floor. I have been given a supernatural baby, the first human being in the history of the world who functions entirely without sleep. If I had the energy, I'd start working on a *Guinness Book of World Records* application.

How can my parents sleep through this? I tear off a piece of paper for Sophie. She wads it and bats it around and grins at me, happier, giddier, and more defiantly pleased with herself with each passing moment.

What can I expect? I've taken this baby from the smells, tastes, and language that defined her world and now I'm even trying to convince her that day is night.

Sophie nods her head in that rhythmic way that causes her to appear enormously enthusiastic and makes kissing noises at me.

That afternoon friends arrive from Nebraska, Iowa, and Missouri, and they gather with my Kansas City relatives for a shower. Dad's videos show me eating lunch, opening presents, talking nonstop, giving Sophie a bottle. The camera sweeps the cake Aunt Gena ordered, with a panda and the words *Welcome Sophie*. The video shows Jody laying Sophie down onto a blanket on the floor, her eyes popping open, her mouth stretching in protest.

Dad is in none of the footage, but sometimes I hear his voice. "Quit pinching her, Jody," he says as Sophie sends up her plaintive wail. He seems so quiet, I wonder again if he's been getting enough sleep, if we've been keeping him up.

My friends tell me I'm a natural, that Sophie and I seem right together. And I hear myself tell Claudia, "She's mine. It's like she's supposed to be mine." I'm surprised to hear myself say this, and even more surprised that I'm not just saying what I'm supposed to, that this is true.

We have to get up early to travel tomorrow. I'm panicked at the idea of trying to navigate airports without any sleep. Mom says she'll stay up with Sophie tonight.

Sophie fusses, so I get up and give her a bottle. When I go back to bed, she steps up her fussing.

I get up to change her diaper. I get up again to turn on the radio. Mom bounces her and sings "Rock a Bye Sophie" over the soft croon of country music and Sophie's yells. I'm never going to sleep in this chaos.

I send Mom to bed and sit up with Sophie again. Maybe I should just let her cry, but I can't, not yet. Even when it's a tearless cry of rage, not fear or need, I believe that rage takes root in unmet needs, and I can't leave her, not yet.

Sophie beats a wad of paper against her head. *Oh, baby, just sleep,* I whisper. Everyone says she'll be fine once she's alone with me and establishes a routine. I'm afraid to get my hopes up.

In a few hours, we have to leave for the airport. Behind their door, my parents sleep on, and I don't know whether I'm grateful or relieved that they aren't coming to South Carolina right away. I'm terrified to be a parent all alone, but it's not like my parents have been able to help much these last few days.

Home. Despite my fears, I can hardly wait to unpack my suitcase, read my mail, wash our clothes, fix my own meals. I can hardly wait to be back in my orderly house among my own things, my own house with the crib all assembled and decorated and awaiting my sleepless child.

ℬ

While I've been away, billboards and banners have cropped up all over Laurens County.

On the highway to campus, I see my first one:

STAR QUARTERBACK.

COLLEGE BOUND.

THE IDEAL SON.

AND A FATHER.

TALK TO HIM BEFORE IT'S TOO LATE.

Teen pregnancy is a big problem here. But my panic reflex can be set off by the most minute things these days. You are not a star quarterback, I remind myself. You are not anyone's son. You are not in danger of dropping out of high school.

But right before I left for China, one of my colleagues said, "I hope this baby won't derail your career." Her words play and replay.

Sophie babbles in the back seat. She has resigned herself to the car seat, the stroller, the high chair, shopping cart seats, and the bathtub, not without some struggle but more easily than I expected.

A banner flaps in the wind near campus:

A BABY COSTS $500 A MONTH.

I frantically start adding it up: diapers, day care, formula, babysitters, clothes, and toys. Then I remember that I've budgeted more than $500 a month, which strikes me as a low estimate.

The next day I pass a billboard on the highway to Greenville, the one sign I can't rationalize away:

HELP WANTED.

NO SICK LEAVE.

NO HOLIDAYS.

NO PAY.

ARE YOU READY TO BE A PARENT?

ℬ

The truth is, I'm crazed, I'm restless, I'm stalled, I miss my old life, my routine, reading, writing, thinking, sleeping, biking, attending exercise classes, effortlessly running errands. Everything is so hard. Sophie is always hungry, wet, or poopy. She's bereft if I step out of her sight for even a second. Music scares her. At least she has started to sleep at night, though she frequently wakes and cries.

I thumb through baby books trying to figure out how to handle the nighttime disruptions. Then I call wise and experienced friends.

"Pick her up whenever she cries," my friends say. "Put her in your bed."

"Pat your baby and tell her that it's time to sleep," the books advise. "Never pick the baby up."

"Oh, no," says Pat. "With adopted children, you should always hold them when they cry. Sit up with her all night if necessary."

I try one thing, then another; I'm a model of inconsistency. Her cries grow desperate if I don't pick her up, but when I do, she flops and twists and leaps. In my bed, she sits up, kicking the sheets and my rib cage. I'm afraid to go to sleep lest she fall off the bed.

My first few attempts at errands last less than an hour, but they take the whole morning to prepare for and the whole afternoon to recover from.

Back when I moved from Nebraska to South Carolina, I was struck by my new ease in the winter. I no longer had to sacrifice my fine motor coordination to so many layers, I no longer had to go out twenty minutes early to defrost the car, I no longer had to trudge through block after block of cold so bitter it brought tears to my eyes as I yanked my feet from snowbanks.

Now, going anywhere with a baby feels harder than the coldest Nebraska winter, more complicated than packing for a camping trip in the Arctic. Check diaper bag for diapers, wipes, spare clothing, and Kleenex, return socks to Sophie's feet, gather snacks, formula, wallet. In and out of the car seat, the stroller, carts, Sophie stiffening her legs each time. Repeated dives at stoplights and under tables for bottles, junk mail, menus, and the Cheerios container.

Most of the time we stay home. At the end of the month-long first week, I call Caroline. I feel like I've been stuck in an elevator for days. The walls are closing in on me. My life is a motionless, airless box.

Caroline speaks in the kind of dead-calm voice reserved for talking others down from ledges. Get the stroller, she says. Take Sophie for a walk.

I do, bumping across pavement, grumpy that there are so few sidewalks.

Kids at my apartment complex have taken to playing in the parking lot rather than the grass. The whole place seems like a way station for people waiting to graduate, buy houses, or move to retirement homes. I am in such a curmudgeonly mood, I wonder why people bother to hang wreaths on their doors at Christmas or now, in summer, decorate with duck-shaped nameplates or arrangements of dried grass. Who was I kidding to think that a baby would make me feel more at home?

We cross the lawn of the nursing home next door. My apartment is only a few feet from the Alzheimer's wing, lots of old people forgetting their pasts. On the other side of the busy highway, I push the stroller through a residential neighborhood where I used to ride my bike. There are no side-walks here, and all the streets are named Sherwood Forest, even the ones that intersect. I push the stroller, walking and walking to cut my tension.

On the way home, I notice how green the grass is everywhere. Someone waves at us from the window of the nursing home. My spirits lift, even if they have temporarily forgotten how to soar.

A newspaper advice columnist tells a bored stay-at-home mom that all occupations are tedious, child rearing no more and no less. Why, even his job, writing columns and books and giving lectures, is more monotonous than glamorous much of the time. I wonder how much uninterrupted time he has spent in the company of children. I'm not a violent person, but as I stare at his smug mugshot I have an irrational urge to slap him. I would be happy to trade my tedium for his.

Even the most boring work of my profession, grading papers and sit-ting through long-winded meetings, appeals to me right now. I would give anything for a morning to work on the novel I've put aside, an hour or two to read a book, a dose of intellectual stimulation and deep concentration. I'm sleeping at night, thank God, but my psyche hungers for the daytime equivalent of REM sleep: daydreams, reflection, free-flowing thought.

I keep waiting for a warm ooze of maternal joy to suppress my ambi-tion, my need to feel like I have a purpose out in the world, to make me less driven and replace the passionate engagement in work that has de-fined my life.

"I am never going to read a book again," I moan by e-mail to my friend Petra.

"Then you will no longer be called Nancy McCabe," she replies. She doesn't take me seriously for one second. She knows me too well.

I call Claire, a poet friend and mother of two. "This is boring," I confess.

"Sort of like Buddhist meditation?" She sounds amused.

"Well, not *that* bad." A few months ago, I dropped out of the intensive meditation workshop we signed up for when it became clear that we were going to do nothing but sit still and breathe for sixteen hours. But just the mention of meditation stirs up longing. It seems like a lifetime ago that I took off on a whim for a meditation weekend, folk concerts, contra dances and cardio-kickboxing classes, weekends biking around Key West and Hilton Head. I was always game to visit an evangelical church or a drag show.

Now I'm supposed to spend my days reveling in the miracle of eye-hand coordination and basic motor skills. Over and over Sophie rises to her haunches and then goes splat as she tries to crawl. After several hours of that, she gets busy pulling her busy box toward her and pushing it away. Then she tears into the junk mail, rattling the cellophane windows. I feel desolate when I imagine a whole summer of watching her eat paper.

We go to campus. In every building, staff members surround Sophie and admire her. We walk around my complex's parking lot, and kids ask me if she's biracial, how long I'm going to keep her, and if she speaks Spanish. She smiles for the crowds, plays vigorously, naps when she's supposed to, splashes in the bathtub, kicks joyously in the stroller, and bangs toys in her crib till she conks out. When I tell friends how crazy I feel, they ask if I regret adopting her.

Are *they* crazy?

Repeatedly, amazement prickles my skin with the power of an adrenaline rush. I went to China and brought back this perfect baby. How did I get so brave? How did I get so lucky?

And what is wrong with me, that this wonder is not sufficient to fill my days?

At an adoption support group meeting, we are no longer a bunch of adults sitting sedately around a room. Conversation has turned choppy as we leap up to intervene in toy disputes, rescue climbing babies from the precipice of danger, change diapers, or root for snacks. A chubby Korean boy toddles across the room, two Chinese girls snatch blocks from each other, and two boys from the Marshall Islands roll a ball back and forth. Sophie wriggles on my lap, wanting to join the fun but wanting to stay close to me. There is only one family left that doesn't have a child. They're leaving next week to get their Chinese daughter.

I want to ask the other moms whether they feel bored and cooped up, but I don't. They are all stay-at-home moms and they might disapprove or find my question condescending. We don't talk about restlessness or monotony or the loss of our identities. Instead, everyone asks me questions about my trip. Instead, we comment on the beauty of all of these children.

I imagine the pages of my novel-in-progress yellowing in a box on my desk. Dust has whitened the shelf packed with books I want to read. My friends send me e-mails about books they just read, and I'm jealous. I receive a notice that one of my poems has been dropped from an anthology.

I hope this baby won't derail your career. I can't chase away my colleague's words. She wasn't referring to my career at the college, which regularly veers on and off track. She was talking about my writing, the publications I've started to accumulate. And now she's right. I can't work. I don't have enough time or concentration to prove her wrong.

Instead I watch Sophie strain onto her arms, groaning and growling as she does her baby pushups. I get down on my hands and knees and demonstrate how to crawl. Sophie thinks that this is funny. I crawl across the floor while she giggles. My brain withers.

The South Carolina summer is upon us, hot and sticky. The registrar calls, wanting my final spring grades. I just picked up the exams yesterday. I'm supposed to have another week. Sophie won't nap. She melts down every ten minutes. Every meal I've tried to eat has been interrupted by some new need, demand, task, or phone call. The neighborhood kids keep knocking on the door to ask if Sophie can come out and play.

"No, she can't come out and play," I say. "She's a *baby.*"

I'm trying to assemble the jumper saucer. I've spread it out on the kitchen floor. Sophie's little hands are everywhere. The plastic pieces I've sorted and counted according to the diagram end up in the wrong piles, under her stuffed animals, in her mouth. The rest of the directions might as well be in Chinese for all of my ability to comprehend. I throw them down. Sophie crumples them and puts them in her mouth.

"Damn it!" I yell, snatching the paper back. Sophie freezes and then a tremor passes through her.

This is how child abuse happens. Fuses stubbed by heat and frustration, body slick with sweat and cheeks burning, how easy it would be to shake or push a child. I pick up my baby and hug her hard.

Late in the afternoon, colleagues drop by with presents. Anita and Jane assemble the jumper saucer. A teenager from the next building plays with Sophie for an hour while I eat dinner and pay bills. Sara arrives by Amtrak early the next morning and cooks fabulous meals and cleans up, changes diapers and feeds Sophie and washes her hair while I grade finals. By the end of the weekend, I am ready to fling out my cramped tight limbs and run through a world that has expanded back to its old size.

Next week, my parents will be here and I'll return to work. I hum and sing and put on Peter, Paul, and Mary. We jiggle plastic keys and rattles to "Leaving on a Jet Plane." We sit-dance to "Puff the Magic Dragon." Sophie growls at her socks as she extricates them from her foot and then howls to "Good Night Irene" like an unspayed cat.

I read an entire novel while she busies herself, as intent as a CEO confronting important paperwork. She studies the back of a *TV Guide* she has ripped apart, crumples up the phone book, bonks a stacking cup against the coffee table, and tries to figure out how to reach another cup that has bounced away. Then she gets distracted by the texture of the carpet. The woolly roughness of rugs, the prickliness of grass, and the furrowed skin of water can hold her entranced for hours.

When I pick her up, she squirms and kicks the air. She wants to be held but she wants, just as fiercely, to be free, to walk and run on her inexperienced legs, and it makes her mad that she can't figure out how. I think about my work, and it's like my blood pumps with more force, I'm so excited, but already, I miss her. I understand, when she whines to be held but then struggles to get down, what it is to be the queen of contradictory impulses.

I fill out the day care forms. We pick up Sophie's immunization form. The day she is eleven months old, she learns to scoot across the floor. Pulling up on her arms, rocking back and forth on her legs, she gets herself stuck under the coffee table. The next day she learns to sit up from a lying position—lifting her head and neck, straining, struggling, trembling with the effort, and finally sitting.

I'm supposed to lament all the things I'll miss while I'm working: the first time my baby crawls, takes a step, says a word. But watching her learn to scoot, I understand that new skills issue dozens of warnings and many false alarms. It's not like babies suddenly stand and walk or open their mouths and deliver the "Gettysburg Address." Sitting around waiting for Sophie to crawl would be like watching raindrops fall, waiting for them to form a lake. It's all so gradual, there's never one moment when you say, "Yep, it's a lake. I'm so glad I was here to see it become a lake."

So even though I'll miss out on some increments while Sophie's at day care, I understand that I don't need to peruse every single raindrop to appreciate the miracle of their accumulation.

The night before my parents arrive and my summer class begins, I rock Sophie. She sucks on her bottle, her arm curling over her head like a ballerina's, then swaying in the air as if conducting music. Her legs push at invisible pedals. In these small gestures I see the dances she will someday do, the music that will someday stir her, the way she will someday ride a bike and feel the wind rushing by as she crests hills and swoops down them. The past month has lasted forever, but we've made it, and I feel poised on the edge of a future where anything is possible as I rock my baby to sleep.

ॐ

The longest I've been separated from Sophie is a couple of hours here and there. Now, without her for whole days, I feel clumsy and confused. My arms ache. I keep hitching an absent weight higher on my hip. It feels weird to be allowed to finish a sentence, and uncomfortable, like I'm testing out a foreign language. I go into my classroom the first day, drop a paper, and say brightly, "Uh-oh!" When a student uses whiteout on a prewriting exercise, I say, "Just keep writing. Don't worry about—" and then a few seconds pass before I remember that the word is *mistakes,* not *boo-boos.*

My parents are taking care of Sophie. In the mornings she acts pitiful when I leave; when I walk in the door again, she chortles and bounces and leans toward me, the Leaning Tower of Sophie, all but doing nosedives into my lap. She doesn't raise her arms like other babies, just quietly leans until she topples. At night she sits on me for at least an hour, often two, to prevent me from leaving again. I try not to worry about the half-done laundry, the half-cleaned kitchen, and my half-prepared classes. I try to ignore the downstairs obstacle course of luggage and portacrib, trike and airplane and boxed shower gifts, all brought by my parents.

Dad shows me the video footage he's taken of Sophie each day. He has patiently trained the camera on her for hours as she sits on a blanket in the living room, playing and babbling. She picks carefully through his keys, examining each ridge and hollow. She studies the keys as if memorizing their shapes. Then, just when she looks most intent, most studious, she lifts up the key ring and bonks herself on the head.

All morning, I teach *The Odyssey* to freshmen. After lunch or between bites of a sandwich, I mark papers in my office. Then I spend two or three hours working on an accreditation project my department dumped on me before they all went off to spend their summers bumming around Europe, reading mystery novels in lawn chairs, and juggling tennis and racquetball dates. I tell myself that it is unprofessional to be so resentful, but I'm still resentful of the hours I spend on sweltering summer days sorting through papers and huddling beside my space heater in pants and a sweatshirt in my frigid building, knowing that even other untenured members of my department have been excused from this project.

I come in for a few hours on the weekends because I'm not getting far enough on weekdays, when I quit by four just so I can shut myself into my office and write for an hour before I leave. My sentences are clunky, creaking forward like a rusty tin man. I know I should be preparing classes, focusing on the accreditation, or going home to my baby, but even burdened by guilt, this stolen hour is the part of the day I most look forward to. Without writing, I am a diabetic without insulin, an asthmatic without an inhaler, a depressive without Prozac. I am unsteady, my brain chemistry goes awry, and I can't breathe. Writing, I am starting to reinhabit my lost identity.

Sophie won't eat when I'm away. When I come home she gulps down mouthfuls of cereal so fast I'm afraid she'll choke. Babies make life seem so simple: if lack of sleep, hunger, harsh words, teething pain, or separation jolt her world so completely, why do we see adult needs as frailties? Don't we too need sleep, regular meals, kindness, options, boundaries, and unstructured time to play?

So I justify my hour each afternoon when I can finally put away my other tasks and sit down at the computer to eke out my few lumbering sentences. I know from experience that if I keep trying, I'm going to find my way to grace again.

My phone rings. It's Flem, the chair of the education department. He's discovered several more time-consuming tasks that need to be completed for our college to be accredited, and he's decided that I'm the person to do them. The idea of yet more work knots my stomach.

"I don't have time," I answer. "You need to talk to my chairs."

My concentration broken, I give up on writing for the day and go home.

I read *The Odyssey* at stoplights, trains, and slow drive-throughs so that I'll have more time in the afternoon to organize notes or edit a rough draft of an essay or chapter. I'm impatient with slow traffic and long lines. All I want is just a little bit of writing time—why is it so hard? I'm becoming a type A personality headed straight for a stroke or a heart attack in my efforts to clear out time to do what most relaxes me.

I'm racing through student journals when Flem calls again to give me further instructions on the additional tasks. "I'm sorry, but I can't do these," I say firmly. "Someone else in my department will have to. Please talk to my chairs."

At home, Mom and Dad coach Sophie to show off her new skills: She can aim a Cheerio so it lands in her mouth three times out of four. She can bite a Cheerio in half. She can practically chin herself on the stereo cabinet. Mom shows me how, if she affixes tape to Sophie's fingertips, tearing it off keeps her occupied for hours. Mom says she used to do this to keep me busy when I was a baby.

Sophie and I visit the day care the week before my parents leave. Sophie sits on the floor next to a six-month-old who lies there imitating a car motor and pretending to steer. He's as big as Sophie, with tiny little eyes and a pointy nose and chunky legs, a baby that makes you realize the absolute absurdity of humanity.

Leaning over to reach a toy, Sophie regards that big sloppy gurgling kicking baby with the same disdain she reserves for Cheerios drenched in peach-banana Gerbers. But she doesn't cry or act scared. She'll be okay here.

The teacher keeps asking me questions—will I have children of my "own"? Why did I choose to adopt?

I tell her that I'm single. I've found that that's an adequate explanation to some people for adopting rather than giving birth.

"Well, she'll make a nice companion," the woman says.

I'm always surprised by the motives people attribute to adoptive single parents—saintliness or vast loneliness, as if a needy, greedy baby could replace adult companionship. I feel like such a weirdo, loving solitude and struggling most with the loss of it.

My new fantasy revolves around sneaking home once Sophie is in day care to take a nap or read a book all the way through.

I'm dodging sprinklers back from class when I see Flem approaching purposefully.

"Hey, did you get the packet I sent you? You need to get going on that," he says.

"You need to send it to my chairs," I say once again, through gritted teeth. "I won't be able to do it."

We're expecting the death of my stepgrandma any day. Dad has brought a suit in case he has to fly home for her funeral. It hangs, wrapped in plastic, in my coat closet.

Dad is convinced that he got food poisoning on the way to South Carolina. He was almost unable to get out of bed at a motel in Alabama. He continues to retire early and sleep a lot.

My dad has often had nagging ailments over the last few years, especially digestive problems that have led him to down so many Tums he jokes about buying stock in the company. We're used to his spells of sickness, and so we shrug them off, along with his persistent tiredness and dry cough.

Because most of the time, he's chipper, regaling me with Sophie stories when I come home. Sophie loves to imitate him, shaking and nodding and waving. When she pounds on her high chair, he imitates her, and she dissolves into giggles. He imitates her laughter and she laughs harder.

One night at dinner, Dad doubles over with a terrible look on his face. Mom and I drop our forks. He straightens up. "I thought I was going to choke," he says. He tries to swallow a couple of times. Then he leaves the table and goes to sit in the living room, motionless. The fish that he complimented only moments before sits practically untouched on his plate.

Mom and I exchange a glance. Dad never complains. He rarely even admits to pain or allows it to disrupt his routine.

I keep waiting for him to come back. The table is littered with empty salad plates, half-drunk glasses of tea, garlic bread crusts and crumbs, and bowls of cereal and pureed fruit I've been spooning up for Sophie. It's getting dark outside. Dad sits, silhouetted by the window, not rising even to turn on a light.

"Has he seen a doctor?" I ask, finally rising to clean up, clearing away dishes, swiping crumbs with a dishcloth, leaving Dad's plate though he shows no sign of returning, though the butter is starting to congeal.

"We'll go as soon as we get home," Mom says.

That night after everyone else has gone to bed, I put aside *The Odyssey* and look up "swallowing difficulties" in *Johns Hopkins Symptoms and Remedies*. Gratefully, I bypass "Esophageal Cancer." He has only two symptoms of that. Everything else on the list is minor, easily curable.

As my parents pack the truck, consult maps, and settle in for their drive home, I'm caught by unexpected waves of sorrow. "We'll see you in August," Mom says. "And when you get invited to do that job in Florida for next summer, just go ahead and say yes. We'll work out taking care of Sophie. What would you think if we bring Sidney next summer?" She would go on making plans forever if Dad didn't roll up the automatic windows and start backing up. The prospect of all of these visits does not fill me with the old dread. Sophie is making our relationship more mellow, I think as I help her wave goodbye, feeling unusually sad at their departure.

Every morning when I bring her downstairs, her head swivels, searching, her eyes passing between the couches and the kitchen chairs where my parents usually sat.

Sophie remains clingy and easily scared. I've taken to smiling big when I run the garbage disposal or the vacuum, feeling like a deranged happy homemaker in my efforts to convince her that loud noises do not necessarily signal danger. At first when I dried my hair she pooched out her lower lip and cried. Now she leaps to my lap and hangs on tight, as if weighing me down so I won't blow away in the dryer's wind.

She does that before her first morning of day care, reminding me of how fragile she still is. When I pry her off me in the baby room she screams, inciting a chorus of baby wails. "All babies do this," the teachers say, pushing me out the door. Cries follow me down the sidewalk.

Twice, I swivel, about to go back, then push myself on toward my car.

Maybe all babies do this, but mine is not all babies. She's a baby with a history of being turned over to strangers. How can I just leave her?

On campus, I run into two colleagues, also mothers. They commiserate with my anxieties, then tell me that I must not leave Sophie more than two or three hours at a time the first week.

I need at least five hours a day if I'm going to finish the accreditation portfolio. I skip my hour of writing, but I'm still miserable with guilt.

The next day starts with the same terrified cry, the same betrayed, desperate expression. The woman who extricates Sophie from me says, "I tell people we have a real live China doll here."

My mouth drops open. I have no prepared response, but even if I did, I'm not going to make myself heard over the screams of my baby and the clamor of the others, once again all taking Sophie's lead. I'm afraid if I say anything I'm going to sound like a hysterical mommy.

My friend Ruth, whose father is Korean American, has told me that she's always despised being called an Asian doll, as if she's a pretty inanimate object without a brain. This was one of the few pieces of advice she gave me: don't let them call your baby a China doll.

I sit in the car, shaking. At work I can't concentrate. A colleague calls and I tell her what happened. She tells me I'm overreacting.

I e-mail Sara, who shoots back, "Ask that teacher if she'd say 'We have our own little black Sambo here. We have our own little Aunt Jemima.'"

I have too much work to do to brood or confront the teacher. If it happens again, I decide, I will call the head of the day care.

Toward the end of June, there's a cool spell. Sophie and I hang out all weekend together. I read and she plays. We read her books. We play music and bang toys. She naps on schedule, eats heartily, and doesn't fuss at bedtime. I know that we're going to be all right.

But Monday she sticks her socks under the faucet and then has a leaky poopy diaper on our way out the door. We backtrack for a clothes change. On the way to school I discover crusted sweet potato all over my shirt. In my office I hurry to get class prepared. The accreditation portfolio looms in a pile on my desk. I haven't even started working on fall classes or lining up visiting writers. I feel muddled, my brain softened by our peaceful weekend.

Sophie doesn't want to eat. At dinner, she thoughtfully chews apple pieces, then returns them to me. She pinches her lips closed against plum Beechnut and looks betrayed when I shovel in spaghetti rings. All she wants is sweet potatoes with cereal. This child ought to have spectacular eyesight and a low risk of heart attack, since every jar provides 640 percent of her vitamin A.

After she's mostly full, she gnaws on a graham cracker, her face daydreamy, eyes starry as she rubs spilled apple juice, spaghetti sauce, sweet potatoes, and plums into her hair. She does this throughout every meal; every day when I pick her up, I just sniff her hair to find out what she had for lunch.

By the time she falls asleep on my shoulder, I'm drowsy and dirty. The house is a mess and I'm so behind on my work. But once again, the weekend's clarity and certainty returns: we are going to be OK.

Mom calls. She took Dad to the doctor today. There, he collapsed, his heart stopped. A helicopter lifted him to St. John's Hospital in Springfield.

Mom sounds cheerful. She says that they're keeping him for tests, but the doctor assures them it's just some treatable digestive disorder. He'll be fine. Mom expects to be home by Friday.

The next day, I deliver accreditation materials to the education secretary. On my way out, Flem snags me. "Hey, I've got another packet for you," he says in his cheery, blustery way that thinly disguises the reality that he's dispensing orders, not friendly requests. "I need your part next week."

How many times have I patiently told him that I cannot take on these extra tasks? How many times have I asked him to contact my chairs? I blow up. "I can't do it," I say. "I've told you that. I have a new baby. I have summer school classes to teach and fall classes to prepare and visiting writers to line up and my own work to do. This is totally outside the scope of what I was hired to do. You need to contact my chairs."

He looks taken aback, as if this is all news to him.

I apologize for my irritation. "I've got a lot going on and I'm away from my baby all day as it is," I say.

"My brother's dying of cancer," Flem says. "I'd like to be with him, too, but I have work to do. We all make sacrifices."

"I'm sorry about your brother," is all I know to say. I leave before I can find words to express my angry whirl of thoughts about his insensitivity, before I voice my new revelation: that the work he wants me to do is piddling and pointless compared to the well-being of my baby. I am not willing to sacrifice that.

I go back to my office and call Caroline. She agrees that the burden of work on me is unfair, that we must do something. She agrees that it isn't right that I'm the one expected to put in all of these hours even though I'm the one with a new baby. She calls Flem to make sure everything is all right, and he laughs and says, "Oh, I've worked with creative people. They may seem flaky, but secretly they're scheming after your job."

I'm aghast that I've worked so many hours every day, steadily and reliably, and have now been dismissed as flaky. I'm shocked that Flem thinks I have the minutest interest in his job. I'm flabbergasted that he has not listened to one word I've said to him. In the end, after a lunch with two of my senior colleagues, discussing possible solutions, they seem so confused about the education department's requirements that I still wind up being the one who spends more afternoons assembling additional materials for Flem.

When I call home on Friday, Aunt Gena answers the phone.

Aunt Gena lives in Kansas City, a couple hours away from my parents' house near Branson. I can't remember Mom saying anything about a visit.

"Is Mom there?" I ask.

"No, she's not."

"Is Dad home from the hospital?"

"No, he's not."

There's a long silence. My aunt is usually a great talker. This guarded, cautious tone is not like her.

"Do you want me to tell you?" Her voice breaks.

"Of course." I look over at Sophie on the floor. She said her first word correctly in context today: "Bye-bye." She is starting to crawl. I save up lists of her new skills for my parents, who are enthralled by each one. I'd expected to update them tonight. Instead, I brace myself, knowing from Aunt Gena's tone that all our lives are about to change forever.

"It's cancer of the esophagus," she says. "It's widespread."

Earlier tonight, reading a letter from a former student, I kept laughing. Sophie didn't know what was funny, but she laughed with me anyway. Now, as I hang up the phone, crying, she laughs, thinking something must be funny again.

Mom calls. They haven't talked to the oncologist yet. She sounds much more upbeat than Aunt Gena, determined to believe that things aren't critical. I want to believe her, to trust the denial that coats her words.

I look in *Symptoms and Remedies* again. "Although uncommon, esophageal tumors worsen rapidly: by the time symptoms develop, the outlook is poor," it says.

The words make no sense. They are just meaningless shapes.

I push on. Esophageal cancer is more common among blacks than whites. Smoking and excess consumption of alcohol are the greatest risk factors. Swallowing lye or corrosive chemicals can also lead to esophageal cancer.

What a relief. Dad is white. He has never smoked. He's a lifelong teetotaler. I've never known him to swallow any corrosive chemical.

He can't possibly have esophageal cancer. The doctors are mistaken.

I read on. Esophageal cancer most affects men, those over fifty, and those with persistent heartburn problems.

My dad.

"Treatment is generally aimed at relieving the symptoms and making the patient as comfortable as possible," I read.

I make lists, everything I need to do to be ready to leave tomorrow, the next day, next week. I hold Sophie, who will turn a year old less than a week after her grandpa turned seventy, less than two days after he was diagnosed with the illness that will kill him.

Oh, baby, I think, rocking. I wanted you to know your grandpa.

After Sophie goes to sleep, I slip out into a fine mist to retrieve our laundry from the dryer. The basketball court and pool are deserted, unusual on a summer night. I'm so used to the sounds I hardly notice them anymore, yet their absence is startling: the heartbeat of a basketball pounding on pavement, the breath of its swish through the net, the splashes from the pool and kids yelling "Marco!" "Polo!" "Marco!" "Polo!" Despite the silence, the night is subtly alive, a spiderweb shimmering in the corner of my doorway, crickets humming low, a cicada warbling.

Someone emerges from the laundry room, cradling a basket, and inside, a sneaker thumps in the dryer. As I gather clothes, Sophie's and mine, I hug their warmth to me.

I want to hold on to the smells of rain and earth, the linty heat of the dryer exhaust, the chorus of crickets and cicadas, and all the things I love. I've been struggling so hard to arrange all the parts of my life so they fit together, to have everything at once without giving any of it up. My baby, my writing, my family and friends, my books and teaching, solitude and company, work and play.

Now, the night around me throbs with life and I'm reluctant to haul my laundry across the parking lot, under streetlights where tiny swirling bugs have been replaced by tiny slanting raindrops, through the mist to my apartment door and into the bright light of all I will have to face.

6

"Don't you remember this?" Dad kept singsonging as we trudged along the pavement at Silver Dollar City. "You used to watch this waterwheel for hours."

Dad claimed that when I was little, we often visited this Ozark theme park. But as the wheel cut through the water in its lazy revolution, I felt no flicker of interest, no stir of memory. How could I have watched this for hours and retained nothing of it? I wanted to believe that if something mattered, it cut an impression in our brains, that at least it left a few wrinkles like the windblown surface of water before me. I wanted to believe that even if I didn't remember the waterwheel, it was the reason I found, say, hot baths or Cheerios at midnight comforting.

We hiked up steep inclines, then chased our feet down them, passing cabins that housed wood-carvers, glassblowers, and spinners. "Do you still like the big cookies?" Dad asked. "You used to love the big cookies."

I looked at him blankly. He was enjoying this, wielding the power of telling me who I used to be. He owned a past I had forgotten, and I was starting to feel resentful that he had the advantage, that I couldn't wrack my brain into recalling.

"Remember the cave?" Dad said. "We must have gone through it half a dozen times." He smiled. He looked smug.

It bugged me that I couldn't remember the cave. That summer day, as the sun flashed and steamed off the pavement, I shivered a little, briefly spooked by what might be stored in my brain that I couldn't remember.

Were the cave's recesses what gave my mind ideas for creating its own hiding places, I wondered, for swallowing things up in darkness?

My parents bought a lake house in the Ozarks in the early eighties, but I rarely visited until 1989, when I moved to Springfield, forty-five minutes away. Mom and Dad were eager to show me the sights, catching me up on what I'd missed. They took me to the Dinky Diner, a restaurant near Reed's Spring Junction that served tiny hot dogs, tiny tacos, and tiny chicken legs. My parents bought me and my little brother tickets to the Shoji Tabuchi Show in Branson, where a Japanese fiddler performed for an audience decked out in pastel polyester and haloes of permed hair. My little brother had just had one section of hair spiked, one straightened, and one frosted. Skull earrings dangled from his triple-pierced ear. He related to me his fantasy that Def Leppard would leap onto the stage with electric guitars.

Depending on whether the number was fast or slow, women in sparkling evening gowns or checked square dance dresses flitted around Shoji Tabuchi, singing backup. During the show's frenzy of changing colors and flashing lights, applause scattered across the theater. The clapping gathered force when waterfalls suddenly came to gushing life at climactic moments in the music, or when lights reinforced plaintive or celebratory notes by dimming, brightening, or rapidly skimming the stage; or when performers ended a patriotic song by suddenly creating a formation that made all their costumes fit together like a big American flag.

On Highway 76, traffic came to a standstill, and the air was sweet with funnel cake and cotton candy. There was never a burned-out bulb in signs for go-carts and bumper cars and miniature golf courses and water parks and 3-D movies, for the Elvis-A-Rama, a hundred-foot mural depicting scenes from his life. Signs for hotels and restaurants and country music theaters throbbed with lights and sparkled with sequins: The Baldknobbers Hillbilly Jamboree, the Foggy River Boys, Boxcar Willie, the Mickey Gilley Theatre. Lights blinked and pulsed and chased each other above the highway. And Dad said, "Don't you remember coming here? Branson wasn't this developed then, but we used to camp and fish down at Table Rock."

But this bright, cheerful, wholesome surface was just that, bringing forth nothing hidden.

There were vague reasons I'd visited the lake house so rarely before that. They had something to do with our family stories that had become as fixed as photographs, but, I thought, discolored by time.

And so the mother bought five ceramic fish to hang on the bathroom wall, I had written in my early twenties, thinking that I was making up a story. *Five fish: two parents and three babies blowing pink ceramic bubbles. Five: the perfect number for a family, she thought. Those five pink ceramic fish would play the same mute game of Follow the Leader across the bathroom walls of every house where the family lived.*

Often the little girl stared up from her bubble bath at the row of ceramic fish. She thought about the stories her parents told about her, all the cute things she'd said and goofy things she'd done, and she pictured all those stories as perfect pink bubbles that had floated from her parents' mouths to settle and harden into fact there on the bathroom wall.

The little girl stared up at the fish on the wall, at the round, perfect bubbles. She took a vindictive glee in poking and pinching the real bubbles before her, watching as they popped and vanished, turning to soap scum on her hands.

Deep down, though, she felt a vague unease at the fragility of bubbles.

When I was a child, my dad had such power over me: remembered me before I could remember myself, could say who I was with the stories he told. In comparison, I knew little about him. "What do you do?" I'd ask him sometimes, wanting to know his job, the name of his work. Other kids' parents were electricians, neurologists, and teachers, but when I inquired about the nature of my dad's job, he'd say only, "It's top secret."

Every morning he went off to Boeing Aircraft's military plant. I pictured someone jumping on box springs, or Ramona the Pest pulling her kindergarten classmate's springy curls. "Boing boing boing," I'd say. Frequently, we saw Dad off at airports and, on his return, rummaged through his briefcase for gifts: Space Needle pens, Statue of Liberty and cable car pencil sharpeners, a gold-plated Sights of Washington, D.C., charm bracelet.

Dad's silence made him seem omnipotent in his knowledge. Once, Department of Defense investigators interviewed our neighbors and my brothers about Dad's work. Everyone was stumped for answers. Dad had no trouble obtaining security clearances.

Once in high school, I tried listing details I knew about my dad as I brainstormed for a character sketch. It came down to one or two of his childhood stories and my own memories. He spent a Saturday every spring fighting the Rototiller into straight lines, plowing up earth, and came in smelling of dirt and grass. Every year he grew things my friends had never heard of, sour green gooseberries and red stalks of rhubarb that he made into pies no one but him would eat. He raised pigeons in the back yard, those musty grayish birds that warbled all the time in their dirt-bald chicken-wire coop. Why pigeons, I never knew, not even the kind you could send off with secret messages, trusting that the birds would eventually boomerang their way home; Dad raised the kind of pigeons exterminated as pests in big cities.

Eventually I asked my dad enough questions about his job to figure out that he wired military airplanes. So he was an electrical engineer, I concluded.

But he would not be pinned down. His degree was in math and physics, not engineering, so though he held a job exactly like that of an electrical engineer, he could not accurately be called one, he said.

When I moved to Springfield, the old roles rapidly restored themselves: Dad was still the Keeper of Secrets, the Guardian of Memory, the Repository of Knowledge. One day I arrived at the lake house and found my mom and aunts and cousins all wearing Band-Aids in the exact same spot directly above their left ankles.

"What's with the Band-Aids?" I asked, and Aunt Gena pointed to a nail sticking out of the couch leg. "Everyone keeps running into it," she said. "I bled. I could sue."

"Your dad won't fix it," Mom added.

"You should watch where you're going," Dad said. "I don't go around running into nails."

Later that day, I too scraped against that nail and blood dotted up along the thin scratch.

None of us made a move to remove the nail ourselves, though.

My parents had bought the lake house and started spending weekends there when I was in college. My brothers, aunts, uncles, and cousins scheduled visits; I didn't. I was busy with classes, my job, and my boyfriend, and increasingly tired of jokes about my intelligence, or lack thereof—jokes that had become family habit. I married young and knew, on the road to my honeymoon, that even then my room was being converted to something unfamiliar. The next time I stopped by, a week after the wedding, my younger brother's stereo blasted against the south wall. The rose-and-trellis wallpaper had been replaced by brown plaid wallpaper and by the bared teeth and spiky hair of heavy metal stars. The closet door hung askew and all the windows had been papered with aluminum foil to block out the sun. A hamster ran mindlessly on its wheel, permeating the room with a vague urine smell. It shook me up, how easily all signs of my presence had been erased. Coming home, sleeping in this room, I'd reach out in the darkness, remembering where my desk, my books had been; blindly I reached out into empty spaces.

Sometimes, Dad brought out the shoe boxes of snapshots, numbered and filed, and I turned through them, mystified by the towheaded little girl, her messy hair like a chick's fluff of down. I had to take Dad's word that that child, arranging dolls and pretending to iron, was me. These domestic activities certainly hadn't proven prophetic, and I couldn't remember ever having hair so pale.

Dad, the documenter of my life, now narrated what I couldn't recollect. You were four, he'd say. We were at Yellowstone. Or: don't you remember the house on Morris? You kids built that snowman behind the garage.

Flipping through photos, I seized on one of my thirteenth birthday. Relieved recognition flooded me.

In the picture, my grimace floats above burning candles. Leaning forward in his chair, my older brother appears positioned to bolt off to something more important. My little brother crouches under the table, using its base as a highway for a colorful plastic toy from a McDonald's Happy Meal. My mom hunches over a textbook, studying.

I still had the diary in which I'd complained about being ignored on my birthday. And here was a picture that confirmed my version of things.

"This is exactly how I remember it," I told Dad, my wonder turning to triumph.

From the time I was eleven, I had kept diaries and journals, and that day I stumbled into a new power. Any family member who claimed that we bought the Bobcat in 1978 or that the trip through Plains, Georgia, was in

1979 could be instantly disproved. Suddenly I, the Dizzy Blond, had become a Keeper of Memory, a Repository of Knowledge to rival my dad. Maybe I was a bit overzealous, obnoxious, even; at any rate, Dad began to look at me bleakly, as if I were stealing from him his parental prerogative.

The first time I visited the lake house, it was deserted on a late-winter weekend; I had grudgingly taken up my parents on their offer to let my husband and me stay there on our way back from Arkansas. We followed my dad's detailed instructions down to Hoot Owl Point and fished out the keys he'd given us.

I halted in the doorway. This was the right house, all right.

There was the old living room couch, the long, muddy-colored yellow couch where I used to lie and read, letting the arm covers slip down to puddle on the floor. There was the old booth-style kitchen table, the vinyl seat torn where my older brother's belt buckle had caught it. The tin dishes we ate from when we camped, my grandfather's flower-stamped silverware, a hideously bulbous lamp had all vanished years ago, discarded, I had assumed. Now, my glance sweeping the room set off eerie pinpricks of memory, the whole past concentrated the way it is suddenly when you bite into a cookie made from an old family recipe, or when you sniff the air the first summer day that someone flips on the air conditioner.

I had long been fascinated by memory and forgetting. I was a sucker for movies and books about amnesia, the kind where a woman wakes up after a twenty-year coma and thinks she's still a seventeen-year-old cheerleader. Or, after a car wreck and two clinical deaths, a woman no longer remembers her own name, recognizes her husband, or even knows what a husband is. I was glued to the page as Sybil suddenly finds herself wandering the streets of strange cities with no idea how she got there. I was transfixed by the story of the woman who didn't speak Russian but claimed to have the same scars, birthmarks, ears, feet, handwriting, and facial proportions as the youngest daughter of Russia's last czar.

I had emerged from consuming obsessions with time travel and with children raised by wolves, gazelles, and apes. For the amnesiac, the time traveler, the feral child, the world becomes a minefield requiring constant negotiation to heal the rifts between familiarity and strangeness. That tension of identity is especially compelling for those of us who always saw ourselves as outsiders: a larger-than-life representation of that experience, but with the startling freshness of a poet's vision.

Now I wandered through my own interval between the past and present, memory and forgetting, the intimate and the unfamiliar. This bedspread, that dresser, these ragged washcloths: I knew the weaves and grains in the same way I knew the lines etched on my palm or the design imprinted on a penny, things I could identify if placed before me but could not, offhand, describe.

Stepping into the bathroom, I stopped short.

As if out of my own imagination, out of a story I'd written or a dream I'd dreamt, four pink ceramic fish swam across the wall. Two parents and two babies blew pink ceramic bubbles.

Shouldn't there be five fish, though? I wondered. Where was the other baby?

Flinging her wet towel toward the rack, the daughter caught instead one of the baby fish on the wall, I wrote, inventing an answer, I thought. *It leapt from its place, crashing to the floor and splintering into five jagged pink ceramic shards. A fin skidded across the tiles to settle against her foot. Then, suddenly, her mother was in the doorway, face white with bright red splotches, the way it got when she was angry.*

"How could you?" She knelt on the floor to gather the pieces with shaking hands. "What is wrong with you?" she yelled at the daughter, who stood dripping in her bathrobe, shocked at her mother's disproportionate rage. "Why do you always have to ruin everything?"

Not long after I moved to Springfield, I saw in the national news a story about a man who was convicted of a crime based on a daughter's long-forgotten memory. Suddenly, everyone was talking about recovering what had been repressed, as if the memory were a graveyard in which what was buried could rise from the dead. The idea haunted me; could we ever really resurrect what had been forgotten?

It was Christmas, and Mom launched into a story: "I remember you were such a little thing," she said, her version of "once upon a time."

I sighed and waited for her to drag out a familiar story, told to me with the exact same words as the last time as if she were on the witness stand. It would be years before I really sympathized with that fierce need to finally pin down the past, that fierce longing to stand firm on our small islands of history while the shores of reality shifted around us.

"You must have been two or three," Mom said. "You were playing in the bathroom and you knocked one of those fish off the wall."

Now I was listening. Goose bumps prickled across my scalp and arms. I didn't remember hearing this story before.

"I can't ever remember being so furious, so out of control." Mom folded the corner of some waxed paper; my mother habitually folds everything, once, then twice, then three times, pleating the pages of books, crafting the church bulletins into fans, leaving waxed paper scarred. When my mother has forgotten everything else, her hands will still remember how to fold.

"I yelled at you and hit you," she said. "And then I thought, 'Why, I hate my own child. This is just a stupid ceramic fish and I hate my own child over it.' I worried that you'd be traumatized forever. Don't you remember?"

I just shook my head. I struggled to picture what I'd described on paper: the clean fish-shaped space on the wall, the fish smashed to scaly shards and pink dust fine as powder. I didn't remember this, really, yet the fish had spent years floating beneath the surface of my memory. Now I waited for that memory to emerge the way fish under ice reappear with the thaw. Nothing came to me, no real memory of that day that I broke my mother's bathroom decoration.

And yet somehow, I had been aware, all those years, of the presence of those fish under that ice, their fleeting movement, their darting shapes.

The knowledge of my parents' inevitable deaths has always flitted like those dark fish, surfacing ten years ago the day my dad lost his memory. That day I was in the middle of moving, transporting and carrying boxes and furniture, and organizing a squad of nine helpers. Dad seemed unusually meek and passive, his eyes glazed, but I was too preoccupied to notice. When he approached me and started asking confused questions, I teased him: "What's the matter, Dad, getting senile?"

It wasn't till later in the day that I understood that something was wrong. The realization dawned slowly, after my friends had gone and my parents and I had set to work unpacking, sorting, and assembling.

Dad had been cross-legged on the bedroom floor for more than an hour, putting together the bed frame he'd bought me. I passed by as he sorted through little Baggies of leftover screws and reread the instructions. Squeezing shut one eye, peering with the other into the box, he shook it.

"What size is your bed?" he asked me.

"I thought it was queen sized," I answered.

He squinted at the instruction sheet for a second, then concluded, "I think it's standard."

"Well, I could be wrong."

It was an inane dialogue, one I wouldn't even remember if Dad hadn't started sifting through the little Baggies again, then reread the instructions and rattled the box. He squeezed one eye shut as he peered into the box with the other, just like he'd done before.

"What size is your bed?" he asked.

Instant replay, a time warp?

"I *thought* it was queen sized," I answered, irritated. I thought of riding my uncle's pontoon, listening to my dad and his brothers converse. *Been fishing yet his year?* asked one, and the others stared out silently at the water until I had forgotten the question. *Haven't had much chance yet,* answered another. The pontoon glided through the water, and maybe somebody grunted. A few miles later, one of the brothers asked, *Is it mostly crappie down here?* And so on: this endless slow-motion small talk.

Now as Dad squinted at the instruction sheet, I despaired. "I think it's standard," Dad said.

We lived in completely different worlds if this passed for conversation, I thought. I was unwilling, unable to fathom that he wasn't deliberately behaving strangely, that the situation was beyond all of our control. After all, Mom seemed calm. She was unpacking the towels I'd wadded into boxes, she was busily refolding them neatly.

I had to escape. When I returned a few minutes later, Dad was in the same position, cross-legged on the floor, scrutinizing the Baggies and then the directions, then jostling the box while he peered in. He raised his head expectantly to me. "What size is your bed?" he asked.

Mom dropped a towel she had folded three times and fumbled to find the labels on the mattress.

"I thought it was standard," Dad said.

"It is," Mom said in a firm voice that should settle the matter. "Here, Bill, you're right. It's standard."

Dad fingered the Baggies. Perused the directions. Shook the box. Same facial expressions, same slightly jerky movements. Looked up as if seeing me for the first time.

"What size is your bed?" he asked me.

"I don't know how many times he's shaken that box," Mom said. "He doesn't remember helping you pack last weekend, either."

"What size is your bed?" Dad asked.

"You already asked me that," I said. Before he could launch the whole routine again, I flung the Baggies and the instruction sheet into the long box and ran to hide it in the pantry. Out of sight, out of mind.

I was shaking. Was there such a thing as sudden onset Alzheimer's? I wondered. Or sudden onset obsessive-compulsive disorder?

During the next thirty minutes I made new discoveries about my own strength and speed, how quickly I could wedge a full file cabinet against the wall or whisk boxes of heavy dishes out of the way. Despite my best efforts, Dad became fixed in a new sequence: he worried aloud that the bed frame would scrape the wall, he squatted to examine it, he rose and purposefully exited the room. Then he wandered back in, worrying aloud, squatting, scrutinizing. These odd calisthenics would continue for hours if I didn't stop them.

"Should we go to the emergency room?" I asked. "Dad?"

"Nothing is wrong with me," Dad said, his tone a familiar, exasperated one.

"You keep forgetting things." I sounded accusing. I felt like I was the one acting crazy, as if I were being insensitive, embarrassing him. Mom was no help. She held herself rigid and shook her head helplessly when I appealed to her. We were used to Dad being the one who took charge.

When he determined to transform part of my desk into a headboard and attach it to my bed frame, my alarm finally outstripped my caution. I ordered both my parents to their car, since mine was still full of boxes. Mom yielded the keys without protesting.

"There's nothing the matter with me," Dad said, but he complied with the air of a courteous but puzzled child, toting along his jacket in one fist.

"Which hospital?" I asked. When Mom didn't answer, I tried again. "Cox South or St. John's?" Mom turned to me, watery eyes wide and defenseless.

As I wove in and out of traffic with my meek and shrunken parents who cowered in corners, I could hardly stand to look at their blank faces, the familiar faces of strangers in a world where everything had reversed from how it was supposed to be. I thought about my dad's photographic negatives, which had always given me the creeps, the way faces and bodies faded to ghosts where they didn't become sharply planed and masked with shadows. Eyes and mouths turned to strange sunken hollows; smiles turned demonic. Often, I had failed to recognize people that I knew.

This car drove easier, smoother than mine: I braked too hard at lights and around corners. Aren't you supposed to be bleeding to go to the emergency room? I kept wondering, worried that I was breaking some unspoken social code, abandoning my manners. Shouldn't a bone have snapped, shouldn't there be unbearable agony? Was it really appropriate to go because someone was repeating himself?

In the rearview mirror, I caught sight of my dad's blank blue eyes. In them I saw how quickly a whole life could vanish, become a slate wiped clean.

Who will mow the lawn? I thought, absurdly. Who would remember me before I remembered myself? My mother's eyes were nearly as empty as my dad's, as if thirty years of marriage had turned my parents so symbiotic that she would be permanently disoriented by his confusion.

Jamming into park in the hospital's circle drive, I raced inside to ask directions to the emergency room. It was starting to rain.

Dad seemed as self-possessed as usual, answering questions at the check-in station. He remembered the year and place of his birth and the name of his insurance carrier. In the waiting area, he cleared his throat in his authoritative way as if preparing to say something wise and provocative; he sat as still as always, fidgetless, patient. Mom folded a tissue, which softened as she worked it. After Dad was called and Mom left with him, I watched the rain fall outside waiting room windows, recalling a day a sparrow flew down my chimney. All day, the bird flitted back and forth across the rooms, battering itself against panes. I, a city child, opened the front door and tried unsuccessfully to coax it outside.

Dad arrived and, talking about something insignificant—the new stoplight at the corner, a favorite restaurant that had closed—he reached out in an offhand gesture and trapped the bird in his hands. He rambled on as he strolled across the room and freed the bird outside, shut the door, and finished his sentence, as if catching and freeing live things were as second nature as my mom's tendency to fold things.

Mom found me an hour after we checked in. Dad didn't remember the year or the president, she reported; the doctor said that he had Transient Global Amnesia, that it wasn't rare in men between forty and sixty. The cause was uncertain, maybe a glitch in circulation that blocked the flow of oxygen to the brain.

Suddenly the memories my dad had always lorded over me seemed like gifts. Someday, I will be sad that my daughter doesn't have the same thing, someone who can remember her before she remembers herself those first ten months of her life.

Hours after he lost it, Dad recovered his short-term memory. Since then, whenever he talks about that day, he says, "It's like I saved it to a bad disk." Nights in my new apartment, I thought of this; I thought of the ceramic fish that had slipped into the shadows of my memory, sending only its small bubbles to the surface. It chilled me that somewhere, with that fish, lay a whole store of experience I could no longer access, and somewhere, with that fish, lay the knowledge that whole lives can disappear, that someday there would be that moment, that phone call, and all at once there would be one less person in the world to remember me, and now, one less person to remember my child. My dad's recovery from amnesia was only a small reprieve, I know this day ten years later as I start preparing to go back to Missouri.

๛

Before the bone scan, my little brother sits up with Dad in the hospital. Dad worries and worries. About his stepmother with leukemia and Alzheimer's. About his ninety-year-old father who drives to sit with her at the nursing home every day. About Mom, who was shaken when they went to visit my stepgrandma. "Promise me I'll never have to live in a place like this," she'd said.

"Make sure she never has to go to a nursing home," Dad pleads with Bob from his hospital bed.

My dad has always assumed responsibility for everyone's lives, my mom for their emotions. This is my parents' division of labor.

The bone scan comes back clean. On long distance, my mom's tone and inflection regain their nuances, her voice rises and falls energetically, and only then do I realize the precise, deadweight way we have formed our words these last few days. Now our voices lilt with hope.

Dad is too old for surgery, but he immediately starts heavy doses of radiation and chemotherapy. I hurry to get things wrapped up in South Carolina. Suddenly I am filled with zeal to go home and be the Good Daughter my parents always wished for. I will transform into the kind of reverent, solicitous daughter they would have liked to have. I will become a nineteenth-century heroine, Beth from *Little Women*, Clara Barton who, in an illustration in a biography from my childhood, wore a bonnet as she dispensed comfort and wisdom. I will ask for nothing for myself. I will be the silent presence who holds things together, pleases everyone, raises flagging spirits, speaks in soft tones, provides freshly mopped floors, plates of sandwiches, and heaps of newly laundered towels. I have never wanted to be this person, but now I do, and so I will. I think that if I can pull it off, I will somehow keep my dad alive.

I buy a plane ticket with an open-ended return date and then immerse myself in wrapping up my summer class, arranging a substitute to administer and mail me the final, and organizing and labeling the accreditation portfolio. I turn it in, and Sophie and I board the plane.

I know it's inevitable that Dad will lose his voice to radiation, lose it forever, that this will be a small price to pay. But that's all I can think of: I want to get home to hear his voice before it's gone. I want to hear him murmur again to Sophie when she screams, "Shhh, you'll wake the baby." I want to hear the way his voice sometimes starts out sarcastic, then gentles at the edges, his exasperated tone when Mom stops listening or worries excessively about something insignificant.

Dad has just been released from the hospital. I bring the car to Springfield to pick him up at my great-aunt's house. It's only been two weeks since I last saw him, and he doesn't look any different, only sounds a little bit hoarse. But as I help gather his clothes and the chemo containers, as Sophie bumps up against the sliding glass doors barking back at my aunt's dog, my mom and dad and Aunt Lee make distracted small talk, too dazed to listen to themselves or each other.

And I buckle down, determined to erase all the ways I've failed my dad. In Aunt Lee's kitchen, I shovel cereal down Sophie and slap together bologna sandwiches for Mom and me. I load the car and then get us all to the pharmacy before it closes. Mom goes in while I buy bottled water for Dad, who scrunches limply into a corner of the back seat. I put up screens to shield Sophie's face from the sun and deliver a banana to Mom in the pharmacy because she keeps forgetting to eat. On the way home, Mom and Dad argue without much conviction or energy about what to do with the empty chemo containers. "It's hazardous waste," she keeps saying. I envision that hazardous waste lurking under the floors, in the basement garage, out in the trash barrels: beneath and around us will be danger, and we will tread over it gently, knowing that our lives are as slippery and fragile as ice. But I concentrate on the road ahead of me and refuse to believe that through attentive housekeeping I cannot rescue us all.

That night Dad gets the hiccups. When I hear the wretched sound knifing through the tissue of his throat, I stop, paralyzed, in the hall outside his room. Sophie hiccups a lot, too, but she thinks hers are funny. Dad's are ragged, wrenching. They rivet me.

Only two weeks ago, Sophie graduated from formula to soft-cooked carrots and spaghetti. Only days after, the doctors found the tumor that would have choked my dad, installed a feeding tube, and switched him to a liquid diet.

Sophie spoke her first word last week, right before radiation began to steal Dad's voice. Sophie started crawling about the same time that the doctors installed a port for the chemo, limiting Dad's mobility. Tonight we came in the door and he stumbled off to bed. He hasn't been up since.

Mom emerges from the bedroom. I follow her to the kitchen, where she eases another can of Ensure from the wrapper.

"Sophie had hiccups a lot at first because I was getting bubbles in the formula from shaking it," I say. "Maybe if you stirred the Ensure instead—"

Mom heaves the can from side to side violently, gives me her now-familiar blank dazed look, and tramps robotically back down the dark hall to the bedroom.

And I stand there listening to the sounds tear from my dad's throat. He is seventy. My baby is a year old. At thirty-six, I am right smack in the middle, briefly a child and parent at the same time. I am the point of intersection, the one who's supposed to be authoritative, in charge.

I have never felt so helpless.

There is so much to do. Bob's children run, feet drumming against the floor. They scream and squeal and whine and fuss, jump on the couch, climb shelves. Sophie bounces and shrieks along with them. Down the hall in his quiet, dark room, Dad lies hooked up to the chemo. Mom mutters to herself, keeping track of feeding times, home health care appointments, and trips for radiation. I mop the floor and prepare meals and wash dishes. Mom is up at six, me at seven, Sophie by eight, Bob's family at intervals between ten and twelve, Jeff at midafternoon. My shopping trip filled the fridge—whole milk for Sidney and Treven, 2 percent for Mom, skim for me, soy formula for Sophie. Bob and his wife, Charlotte, have brought milk formula for Megan; it's piled on the counter next to the Ensure. I have to unload the whole refrigerator to locate one item.

Everyone wants lunch. "Chicken noodle butt soup," Sidney orders, laughing raucously. Treven nods vigorously at the peanut butter jar. I mix vegetables and cereal for Sophie and formula for Megan. Mom's back for more Ensure. Dad calls it Endure and says he feels stuffed all the time. I make Mom a plate with a ham sandwich and some grapes.

The kids' noise makes me anxious. I don't know how much is leaking into Dad's room. Once or twice, when everyone is calling me at once, I have to stop, cover my ears, and close my eyes. I doubt that Florence Nightingale was ever tempted to put her fingers in her ears and growl to drown out the demands of others.

Charlotte and I let in the home health care nurse, wash dishes, and herd the kids away from Dad's room while Bob mows grass and cuts firewood down at the lake house. Two-year-old Treven's being a little caveboy, pointing and grunting when he wants juice or crackers, regaling me with a beatific smile when I tell him to keep his juice in the kitchen or quit climbing on the back of the couch. He likes to lift the babies by their armpits and haul them around, grunting proudly as if to say, "I big. You little." He points and grunts at a box of Lucky Charms three times in one morning. Three different people pour him bowls of it. When I gather dishes to be washed, I find full bowls of soggy, disintegrating cereal, colored marshmallows melted into pastel pools.

Along the road, big tents sell fireworks, like it's a holiday or something. On the Fourth of July, my brothers and Charlotte and the kids and I watch traces of distant fireworks from the other side of the bridge. Dad stays in his bed hooked up to the chemo. Mom shakes and peels open cans of Ensure. We watch colors burst above us and then the long trail of blue and white lights down on the lake, boats cruising back from watching the show.

Dad is so weak that he falls on his way to the bathroom. Later, I glance into his room. Mom is feeding him through the tube. He looks gaunt in there flat on his back, eyes swollen and reddish. My brothers go in to talk to him sometimes. While I feed kids and clean up messes and try to keep the small tribe from getting too rowdy, I hear Jeff and Bob and Dad engaged in long conversations about the holiday traffic. Sometimes Dad asks to see Sidney or Sophie, but never me. I don't know what we'd talk about anyway.

"It makes me sad to see you sick, Grandpa," Sidney says.

"I know it does, Honey," Dad says.

I try to remember being so young and earnest, so able to find words.

All night Sophie kicks at her blankets. "Mama, mama," she murmurs in the dark. She wakes with diarrhea. I strip her bedclothes. I feel cramps coming on. I have no supplies and no idea where I've packed the ibuprofen.

The kitchen floor is sticky no matter how often I mop. The air conditioner fan won't come on. Swallowing bites of breakfast, Sophie coughs then gasps soundlessly. I snatch her up, tipping her sideways. Gruel comes up, carrot-peas with rice cereal. As Bob's family heads out the door, back to Kansas, I clutch Sophie tightly, shaking. And then get back to work.

The house's temperature rises a couple of degrees every ten minutes. Mom and Jeff are getting ready to take Dad to Springfield for radiation.

"You can't bring him back here," I tell Jeff. "It's too hot. Get Mom to pack a bag and stay at Aunt Lee's so he'll be comfortable."

Jeff doesn't answer. He goes off to the bathroom. Mom comes in for her purse.

"Mom," I say. "You can't come back tonight. It's too hot."

Mom ignores me. Dad walks himself to the car. We all watch tensely. Then Mom and Jeff slip into the car and pull away. Up until the last minute, I'm sure one of them will regain their senses and come back for an overnight bag.

Sweat trickles down my face and trails between my breasts as I shuffle through the phone book. All morning, Sophie's hair has been soaked with perspiration. I open windows, but there is no breeze. My parents shouldn't be driving back and forth to Springfield. The trip causes additional stress for Mom, additional discomfort for Dad. And what if they have car trouble?

I call every air conditioner repair shop in the Branson area yellow pages and leave messages. Sophie reaches up to grip an end table. She pulls herself up. She's standing. She's standing for the first time.

No one returns my calls. I get back on the phone. I call appliance repair services in Springfield. I plead. I tell them that my dad is terribly ill, that he's dying, that the house is ninety degrees. Some just don't have time. Others sympathize but tell me that it will take at least a week to get the right part.

I wait for the phone to ring, Mom or Jeff telling me that they're staying in Springfield. Instead, late in the afternoon, the car pulls into the driveway.

I meet Jeff at the door. "How could you bring him back here? It's too hot."

Mom comes in behind him, flinching. "It's cooler in the basement," she says. "I can give you some fans to take down there."

Dad stumbles in, sends me a look of pure disgust, and hobbles to his room.

Once when I was a kid, a wayward ball from a neighborhood game slammed me smack in the nose. At first, there was nothing but spinning, lights, a constellation of cartoon stars, then bewilderment, and finally pain that vibrated the cartilage of my nose, so my hand flew up to cup it, to contain the pain. I opened my eyes and I was still standing there, it was still daytime, the game went on around me.

Mom's words hit hard like that, a shock and then a diffuse pain. Unlike a wallop to the nose or a punch to the gut, the pain does not shrink to be contained finally by one area: it expands. They think I'm complaining because *I'm* hot. This is how they see me.

"I don't want the fans," I say. "I'm not worried about us. I'm worried about Dad. He needs to be comfortable." I wonder if I, too, wear the permanent vacant, stunned expression of the rest of my family. They stare at me as if stoned in the face of their grief and my urgency.

I go downstairs, remembering all the times my family has condemned me for being selfish and self-centered. Many times my parents have sighed loudly because I wouldn't consent to sleep on the couch while the spare bedrooms went to my brothers. Many times my parents have been offended by my feminist opinions, until I finally learned to say nothing when they started condemning abortion rights or making fun of women politicians. Many times my parents have been hurt by the briefness of my visits since, unlike my brothers, I supposedly have summer vacations, never mind that I spend most of them working. But greedy, self-centered, thoughtless? I can't think of anything I've done to earn this reputation.

This is the last thing I want to be thinking about right now, but I can no longer resist the knowledge that I gave up trying to please them a long time ago because I could not be the kind of daughter they wanted me to be and still be myself. My parents speak of both of my grandmothers, long dead, in reverent tones: they were saints, kind, capable peacemakers. They turned the other cheek. They spoke no ill of others. My mother wants to be remembered as a saint. "Blessed are the peacemakers," she used to say to me, repeatedly.

"But Mom, don't you want us to remember you as an interesting person?" I used to ask. "Someone with a personality?" She didn't.

Against these models, how can I ever seem to be anything but hopelessly selfish?

But I'm too desperate to give up completely. "Why don't you move to the basement?" I ask Dad. "It's unbearable up here."

"It'll cool off after dark," Dad says, staring at the ceiling. I can barely hear him. He asks me to water the plants, tries to tell me which ones, but his voice is so quiet I can't make out his words and I don't want to wear him out by forcing him to repeat them.

I overcompensate. While Sophie naps, I water everything, even the scraggly growth in the log-lined beds that might be weeds. I haul a bucket up and down the sloping backyard to drench the flowers the hose won't reach.

"Did you grade your finals yet?" Mom asks me when I come in. I've been on the phone all day to repair services. I've been taking care of Sophie. I haven't even opened the manila envelope of blue books that arrived today.

"You don't need to pay for your own food," Mom says. "I left you some money on the buffet."

There, I find a ten-dollar bill. "You mean this?" I ask.

Mom looks. "Yeah," she says.

I've paid for groceries for everyone all weekend. Between supplies and the cost of a last-minute plane ticket, I'm out of money and relying on credit cards. Every penny I earned from summer teaching is gone. I refuse to worry about the money, though. I'll get caught up in the fall.

But I feel defeated when I look at the ten-dollar bill, this shadow of a gesture from an old life in which my parents paid for restaurant meals, groceries, admission fees, and hotel bills during every visit or family trip. It always embarrassed me a little, but especially when I was in school, I was also grateful. This ten-dollar bill is an announcement that my life as an indulged daughter has ended forever, that a whole way of life is gone. That I am irrevocably an adult.

The next day, Mom, Dad, and Jeff head off to Springfield again. I do all the laundry, grade my finals, and admit the kind air conditioner repairman who drove two hours to get the necessary part. Soon we can breathe again. Sophie's hair finally dries. Her appetite returns. I'm weak with relief that Dad won't have to come home to a blast furnace.

Off to fax my grades, straining to see around Sophie's car seat, I bash the truck's rearview mirror against the garage wall, smashing it. I call the Toyota dealer. He needs the model number. Coming back from the garage, I track oil on the carpet.

The harder I try, the more of a mess I make.

Sophie is tired and prone to meltdowns all afternoon. She sits in the portacrib for two hours without napping. I fold and hang the rest of the laundry while she wails. And then I lift her out of the crib, sink down to the couch, and decide to go home.

I have moved twelve times in the last sixteen years, four times to new states where I had to make whole new lives for myself. I completed a Ph.D. in record time. I have worked sixty hours a week for the last three years and taken on dozens of freelance jobs to earn money for the adoption. I've never missed a deadline or failed to complete a task. If I could manage all that, why can't I take care of a few people? My limitations feel like a drawstring pulling tighter and tighter around me. The evidence of my inadequacy keeps mounting: the shattered mirror, the oil on the carpet, my drained bank account, Sophie's regular screaming fits. Fear has made me delusional: I'll never be the perfect daughter and still be myself. But there's a chance I can figure out how to be a good enough mother and be myself, too.

Mom calls. After Dad's treatment, his eyes glazed over, pupils fixed. The hospital, only a parking lot away, sent an ambulance.

The doctor diagnosed an infection and checked Dad in.

If only he hadn't spent the night in this hot house. If only I'd found a repairman faster. If only Mom and Dad didn't feel obligated to keep coming back here every night, not just seeking the comfort of their own things, I suspect, but also in the grip of the old, polite habit of returning because they have company. I call the airline and arrange our flight home.

That night, I hear Mom on the phone in her study, quoting Bible verses. If it's Dad's time, she'll accept God's will, she says.

Why is she so calm? Shouldn't she be denying, bargaining, getting mad?

But I understand that the Bible verses are her denial, her bargaining. She's steeled for the worst because by comparison reality is never as bad. She's saying, but look, I'm devout, I have faith, so this can't really happen to me.

I wake with a sinus infection. I'm stuffy and light-headed. I lie down again while a million stars shoot out from my brain like little electric shocks, and then I slide down that charged galaxy into sleep.

I try to shower, dress, pack, and clean before Sophie wakes, but I'm dizzy and sluggish. I organize the suitcases, make a lunch for Sophie, and whip up a breakfast of sweet potato spaghetti. She won't eat and we have to go. Mom scoops up Sophie's gruel into a cup so I can feed her in the back seat. Within minutes her hands, face, and clothes are spackled with pureed sweet potato.

We stop at the hospital to say goodbye to Dad. He's sitting up, an improvement. Suddenly he looks so old, angles and hollows of his face exaggerated—ridge of brow and craters of eye sockets and curve of nose. It is as if illness has pared him down to his essence, no soft tissues left to smooth the edges.

I don't hug him goodbye. I'm afraid of giving him my cold. He looks at me as if my mere presence wears him out. Then he turns a tender and sad expression on Sophie, waving to her as we leave.

We dash to the airport, detouring by a drive-through for a hamburger and Coke since I won't have a chance to buy lunch anywhere else. At the drop-off, Mom hurriedly heaps my luggage on the sidewalk. She apparently means to just leave me here.

Many times in the past, Mom and Dad insisted on parking the car and seeing me off at the gate even though all I wanted was some time alone. Now I can't possibly get anywhere without help and Mom's too distracted to notice.

"Um, Mom," I say. "I can't carry all of this." Mom looks surprised but she wheels the luggage in while I heft Sophie and nudge along the stroller piled with the diaper bag and my lunch, Coke wobbling and threatening to spill. Mom asks a family behind me in line to help me and then she is gone, leaving me lightheaded with a fussing baby and a tumble of bags and suitcases. I empty the stroller and deposit Sophie in it so I can kick the baggage forward while I down some cold medicine, take a few bites of hamburger, and throw away the rest of my lunch before we reach the check-in counter.

The trip takes forever—hot small planes, lots of stairs, so I have to keep unlatching Sophie and lifting her out, folding then unfolding the stroller while I try to balance the diaper bag—why is it so heavy? I thought I packed only the minimum necessities. I'm starved and congested, and Sophie keeps yanking off her socks with her teeth, and my glasses fall apart so I arrive in Greenville half-blind. My luggage and car seat do not arrive with me.

It's not till Sophie's in bed that the image of my dad's face flashes back, the way he turned away from me with such grim weariness.

Will this be my last memory of him?

Last Christmas, I burned myself on a glass measuring cup full of boiling water. I shrieked as I took it out of the microwave and sent the cup skittering across the counter.

Dad raised his eyebrows. "Did you burn yourself?" He reached toward me and unthinkingly I gave him my hand to inspect the way I did as a child when I hurt myself.

He backed away. I realized he'd been reaching for his juice.

Things were so much easier between us when I was a little girl, before I was old enough to have my own passions and opinions, my own complicated needs and desires and moods.

I think about the way his eyes followed Sophie from the hospital room, how uncluttered his affection for her is.

Once, long ago, maybe he looked at me like that, some time too far in the past for either of us to remember, that tenderness lost somewhere in the frozen ice of memory.

When I needed an author photo a couple of years ago, Dad shot a series of portraits. In the end, I didn't use them. I couldn't even bear to look at them. Compared to the ones taken by a studio, my face looked too close, too wide-open, too vulnerable. In some indefinable way, I looked like someone's child.

And yet now those photos are my only recent evidence that my dad's gaze at me, his adult daughter, sometimes softened. I thought that my own baby would thaw the layer of stiffness between us. Over time, she would have. Already I've seen a glimpse of how the ways we've disappointed each other would have receded in our memories. I've seen how his ambivalence toward his ambitious, educated daughter might finally have shifted to approval. But it's not going to happen. There is no time left.

What I have left is how his gaze recoiled from me then turned with utter love onto my child. What I have is the way his devotion shone in his eyes as he waved at her, saying goodbye as if for the last time.

7

In the mornings, we wake up excited. Sophie can stand, and from her new elevated perspective, edges jut out at different angles and her world reshapes itself. She chortles with glee at viewing the tops rather than the undersides of tables and shelves. Her eyes are alive with new revelations.

I am writing again and the drab world brightens, colors and flavors intensifying, my mind racing with associations and metaphors.

The first time Sophie drinks from a sippy cup, she kicks her feet, thrilled at mastering another skill. The final strands of my novel are coming together and I'm high on adrenaline, pumped up as I push to the finish, as if my heart kicks its own feet.

Sophie squats from a standing position to pick up toys, balancing unaided. Sentences pour out of me I didn't know were there. I see, finally, how to develop a section. I light on a detail that's eluded me. In the mornings and evenings, Sophie and I infect each other with our high spirits, passing energy back and forth, an electricity of discovery.

When she's promoted from the infant room to the waddler group, seven Olympic gold medals couldn't make me prouder. I count the days I have left before the new semester starts, resenting all the interruptions and errands that hack away at my time.

Sophie wakes with rivers of snot pouring from her nose. I tease her about toting barges, white-water rafting, or taking Princess line cruises through the incredible waterways she's producing. I make up a story about a Slimy Grimy Tot with Snot who meets an Icky Sticky Ogre with Boogers. Sophie has no idea what I'm babbling about, but she giggles anyway. How could this cute baby produce so much mucous?

The infant teacher suggests an antihistamine. The pharmacist advises me to let it run. The day care center director suggests a cork. The doctor calls in a prescription.

When I arrive the next afternoon to pick up Sophie, the director calls me into her office. I squeeze into the rocker seat between a giant Pooh bear and a Tickle-Me Elmo. She leans forward across the desk, very serious and hushed. "Sophie is pulling out her hair in clumps," she says.

My heart arrests midbeat. Oh, my poor baby. Buried in my work rather than staying alert to her every need, I've somehow failed to notice signs of her imminent breakdown. Here I thought we were doing so well, when in fact I've been neglecting her. Now I've put her through one transition too many, moving her up to the waddler group just when she was used to the infant room.

I picture her scalp, now smooth except for a few remaining unruly thatches. I imagine her crouching in the waddler room, on a carpet of dark hair, keening and snarling like a small vicious animal so that day-care workers skirt a wide berth around her. How long will it take her hair to grow back? Will she need a wig? What's next—skin carving? Toddler bulimia? I know there are therapists trained to get at the roots of psychological trauma in babies. I will find one immediately. I will give up my selfish ways, stop assuming that she's happy just because I am. I'll stop writing if necessary.

I sweat profusely as the center director cruises the Internet for information about hair pulling. It's all I can do not to bolt from the office and crash through the building to gather up my poor bald Waddler.

When I finally seek out Sophie, it's at a fast walk bordering on a sprint. I find her cheerfully pounding on a toy keyboard, and I am genuinely surprised at her full head of hair, no visible thin spots or dimes of bald scalp.

Manically she bounces, pounds, and sings, turning toward me with glazed eyes. I instantly know what's wrong. I am instantly flooded with relief: the problem has nothing to do with stress, neglect, selfishness, or mental health crises.

"She hasn't napped," I say.

The teachers confirm this.

"It's her prescription," I say. At home, I check: despite the information in Sophie's chart, the medication has an antihistamine, which has once again exhausted and wired her so she has spent the day tugging at her hair to keep herself awake.

I give her a bottle till she sleeps, then page through baby books gathering advice. When she wakes I give her a stuffed dog and help her pull on its hair. I select a longhaired bear to take to her crib at day care. I call the doctor and ask for a new prescription.

Mom calls. She and Dad have moved to a room near the hospital. They eat in the cafeteria and someone brings a wheelchair to take Dad for his treatments.

I should be deluging Dad with videos and e-mails documenting Sophie's new skills. I know these are the things that will give him pleasure. But then I worry that those things would stress out my mom because she's terrified of technology, and I resolve to send lots of photographs and letters instead. But my list of things to do keeps lengthening. I'll write my parents at the end of the summer and in the fall. Dad's doctors have planned a treatment schedule through November. In a couple of months when he's really weak, he'll especially need my gifts and notes.

Sophie's green card arrives in late July. She's a permanent resident of the United States till 2009.

I apply for her social security number. Although years ago my marriage license automatically allowed me to change my name on my social security card, an adoption decree does not carry the same privilege. Unless I legally change her name, she will be known throughout school and by personnel offices of her employers as Ni Qiao Qin. That will be the name called at her high school graduation. Though she is my daughter, she does not legally share my name or citizenship.

The heart monitor records a too-fast beat and Dad lands in the hospital again. The radiation treatments halt until his heart can be brought under control.

Working out at the Y, I am the aerobics class weirdo. The others wear bouncy cotton shorts and oversized T-shirts with soft drink and radio station logos. They arrive gossiping about recent Mary Kay parties and jewelry shows. They all stack several steps into one monster step with the goal of turning their glutes to jelly. They pile weights onto their knees during squats and choose huge bright plastic dumbbells for lifts.

I use one step and a set of small, light weights. I wear old bike shorts and a too-short T-shirt advertising a literary magazine. I'm the out-of-sync minimalist with the funny accent, no wedding ring, and a Chinese baby. I *so* do not fit in. I will never fit in.

But looking in the mirror at my oddball self, I realize that I am happy. Really happy.

I drop by campus to pick up my annual evaluation letter and meet with the dean. Knowing my employers, I don't expect even minor accolades, but maybe some faint praise for my positive student evaluations and long list of service work and publications. I do kind of hope to be commended for finishing the accreditation project despite my own department's desertion, my new baby, and my dad's illness.

So I'm flattened by the scolding tone of the letter, the rebuke for flouting authority and being confrontational toward a hardworking department chair. The dean concludes that I might as well forget an early tenure bid.

I ask the dean for an explanation.

"Think about it," he says mysteriously.

I tell him that if he's talking about my encounter with Flem, he hasn't heard my side of the story. But I know it's too late. I've already been condemned.

"In the South, we have a tradition of civility." The dean launches a speech about the kind, compassionate way that southerners deal with each other as opposed to my more direct and abrupt midwestern way.

"So should I look for another job?" I ask.

"Well, you might keep your options open. But no, don't give up on this one. I still envision you as an old lady retiring from here."

I'm up half the night, confused and anguished. I pace, staring out at the dark parking lot, write in my journal, examine my conscience, try to figure out what I've done wrong and find some way to repair the damage. In the next room, Sophie mutters in her sleep. Without a job, how am I going to take care of her?

As the hours pass, my anger grows. The letter seems disproportionately harsh. This wasn't supposed to be the result of my soul-searching: I was supposed to come out on the other side humble and meek, because isn't anger my problem? The message from the dean was clear—southerners don't get angry. But what about all of those times that my department members have yelled at me for violations of policies I didn't know about? It's not southerners who don't get angry, it's women.

I've disappointed my parents and now I'm failing at my job. There must be a pattern, a terrible flaw in me that I must root out and squash. I pace and try to figure out what that is. Would others have just meekly accepted the extra work Flem kept dishing out? Would doing so have made me a better person?

I've read that we keep recreating the circumstances of our childhoods, even if those circumstances are traumatic ones or represent values we think we've rejected. Something in us gravitates toward the familiar, mistaking it for comfort.

When I was a teenager, my dad used to sit me down and explain, with thorough, firm logic, why my pacifist views were naive or why the ERA was an insult to existing constitutional protections. With no intellectual defense for my views, guided primarily by emotion and impulse, I shrank in the face of my dad's angry rebuttals. So now here I am at a church-connected college in the South, where I have regularly felt diminished in the same way. I am more articulate now, but I often feel like a radio station not on anyone's dial. Whatever I broadcast, all they hear is static.

In meetings when women speak, the eyes of male colleagues glaze over, or our words are later attributed to men. The men use each other's titles, calling one another Dr. McAslin and Dr. Carothers and Dr. Compson while addressing female colleagues by our first names. One man announces in a discussion of a book on pedagogy that female professors should be expected to be more nurturing—after all, we're the ones who have babies.

One recent noon at the dining hall, a male colleague lectured me about why the inferiority of women was a legitimate theological perspective. Gently he bulldozed every response I offered until I was in tears and mad at myself for not being cooler, more rational and articulate.

What am I doing here? I have been so focused on adopting my baby and doing my job, I've ignored the mounting evidence that I'm in the wrong place, mostly out of a profound disbelief that educated people could hold such outdated views. And now, with this letter from the dean, formerly

one of my supporters, it has become clear that what I've failed at is southern womanhood.

I leap to my feet.

Thank God, I think.

I see you as an old lady retiring from this school, the dean said.

I shudder. And in that moment, I break through anxiety and self-
flagellation to a pure, clean, refreshing anger. I don't want to retire from
here. I can't spend my life being a Good Girl, ever more obedient and self-
effacing, any more than I can manage the Good Daughter role.

I don't want to live my life that way, but even more, that is not a legacy
I want to pass on to my daughter.

Jody has pointed out that adopted Chinese girls are often so docile because they haven't learned to want anything: to survive, they passively take
what is given to them. Somehow, Sophie kept her strong will despite the
odds. Whenever I am exasperated with her, I remind myself that this is the
fierce spirit that survived an orphanage, desires intact. This loud voice got
her what she needed.

I will not dishonor the gift I have been given, this ferocious little soul,
by trying to tame her into a sweet, submissive girl.

We are not going to stay here. But then reality closes in: where am I going to go in this academic job market? Won't another job have some of the
same pitfalls? What if I make the same mistakes? And how am I going to
find another job in another region and move us both by myself?

Every day for the next week I draft a letter to the dean. The tone is schiz-
ophrenic, respectful and meek one day, confident the next, and then, oh,
dear, downright confrontational. I revise it, toning down, then am off
again on an enraged roll. I scale back to merely authoritative. But any attempt to claim authority will be seen as insubordinate, so I put away the
letter so I can cool off and get some distance. Then I take it out and ob-
sessively revise some more.

I abandon my novel. I stop sleeping and eating. I don't take pictures of
Sophie or write to my dad. I write and rewrite the letter, trying to figure
out how to save my job.

Sophie can clap her hands now. She dances wildly to a headbanger version of "I Love Trash" on one of her CDs. I hug and kiss her and tell her
what a lucky mommy I am, and she smiles and snuggles down into her
crib without a fuss. I watch her sleep. I think about my dad whose heart

has been stabilized. He has resumed chemo and radiation. A loose thread on Sophie's pajama sleeve rises and dances like a mesmerized snake in the breeze from her breath, falls limp, lifts again, and all of my conflicts seem silly and petty in the face of my father's ravaging illness and my baby's sweet sleep.

Early Friday morning, the phone rings.

"Dad's not doing so well," Mom says. Last night, he was shouting and groaning in agony—my dad, who stoically bears all pain. The cancer is massive. He has pneumonia and congestive heart failure.

The best the doctors hope for is to make him comfortable. This morning Mom said goodbye to him. This morning Mom said to him, "Bill, I'll see you in heaven."

Dad wakes when I enter the room. Before he abruptly retreats back into sleep he greets me in a strange voice, thick and slow. His face is that of an unfamiliar old man, jaundiced, slack-jawed, hairline receded from the treatments, only a few tufts remaining. Gone, forever now, is the curl that used to swoop low over his forehead. When he slicked it back, it used to stand up like a rooster's comb.

I hold his hand. I have not held his hand since I was a little girl. "How are you?" I say, and feel foolish.

Mom has been sleeping in the chair next to him. The room's dimness erases the fine lines from her face. It is regal, like something carved from marble.

In his gasping, fragmented voice, Dad worries about the whereabouts of the children. We keep reassuring him: Bob's are with Charlotte at the lake. Sophie is with Jody at the hotel.

The next day, the waiting room is like a family reunion of cousins, aunts, and uncles I haven't seen in years. I wonder what Dad makes of all the commotion.

His room goes quiet when Grandpa arrives. He's ninety, frail and sad, and no one told him till today that his oldest son was dying. He stands holding Dad's hand, then stumbles tearfully to the foot of the bed. I touch his arm. He ignores me. We've never been close. I am the granddaughter who was never flirty and giggly. I was the one always buried in books. Now I am the granddaughter hoping that I never have to stand at my own child's deathbed.

"He's still got a grip," Grandpa says hopefully.

Dad claws at the air with both hands.

"Bill, do you need something?" My uncles and brothers spring to attention.

But I know what he's doing: he's showing off his grip.

When I take Sophie into his room, he waves and calls to her. The old man with waxen, yellowish skin and a newly doubled chin becomes my dad again in that moment, the man who can be subdued and awkward around adults but turns silly and gentle and patient with his grandchildren.

Sophie is unfazed by his thick voice or the oxygen tubes hooked over his ears and attached to each nostril. She swipes at and misses the keys on the stand next to his bed. She leans down toward him, hands outstretched.

Dad reaches up. His fingers brush hers like God passing life energy to Adam.

Then he snaps his fingers. The sound is weaker than his characteristic gunshot snap, a sound loud enough that I could always find him in a busy department store or crowded convention center when I was lost as a child.

I don't know that this is the last time I will talk to him before regular morphine doses slip him into a coma. I don't know that this is the last time I will hear him snap his fingers and know that when I am lost, this is how I will find him.

In a strange dream of a night, my mother and brothers and I huddle under white blankets in the chilly dark room. A sunflower on the sill stands tall only because there is no sun to strain toward.

Outside the window, a searchlight blooms and scans the sky.

After a day at the hospital, I went out to dinner, imagining that Dad had days left, that he would fade slowly and gradually. After all, the nurse seemed so offhanded earlier, pitching an empty Ensure can into the trash and saying, "That's lunch." After all, Dad asked me earlier for some hot chocolate and even though he was delirious, the request was enough for me to believe he might still make a miraculous recovery.

But then the doctor hooked him up to the pump that releases morphine every fifteen minutes. Then, while I was gone, Dad shooed away the nurse who came to feed him.

"You have the right to refuse nourishment," she said before she packed up and stole away.

So I came back to a changed atmosphere, hushed except for each of Dad's shallow breaths, an awful labor as fluid gurgles through his lungs. When we hold his hands, he no longer squeezes ours.

"He grew up with only brothers," Mom says. "He didn't know what to do with you. You taught him how to be a father to a little girl and a grandfather to Sidney and Sophie." She turns to Charlotte. "He didn't get much time with the other kids, but he adored them, too."

All day I've been thinking Stop! Don't! When my uncles sat by Dad's bed talking about upcoming fishing trips, my anxiety mounted. Don't! I kept thinking. Don't talk about the future. Would they eat in front of someone starving? When the nurses came to inject Dad with morphine, I wanted to leap up and shout Stop! Don't do it unless he insists. Don't help him die any faster than he has to.

And now when Mom talks about Dad in past tense, I'm seized by another small panic: Don't! I think. He's still alive. He's still listening.

But I understand: she's letting him know that we're letting him go.

We take turns pushing the button that speeds away both pain and life, delivering extra morphine when Dad groans. The pump clicks softly, regularly, drowned out by that inhuman sound of pneumonia in the lungs, like a coffeemaker brewing all night.

Earlier today, Dad kept counting aloud, a side effect of the heart medication, Mom said.

"One, two, three, eleven, twelve, thirteen," he'd say, skipping numbers like a small child. It's as if he's counting toward death the way I count toward sleep on nights that my heart and brain race so fast, I have to focus to calm them. I count, picture colors, wait for images to follow. I concentrate on numbers, colors, and images to replace the barrage of daily details.

In the eerie stillness, I listen to the widening spaces between my dad's pained breaths. All summer I've been listening to breathing. I've wakened Sophie when I couldn't hear the soft sibilance of her breath through the monitor. Once or twice I pulled over the car to make sure her chest was still rising and falling. And now, I lean in to these slow, tortured breaths, forgetting to exhale as I wait for my dad to breathe in again.

I try to focus. One, two, three, blue. The sky. My eyes that are his eyes. Seven, eight, nine, blue. The powder blue Impala he bought in 1963. Blueberries, cornflowers, gladiolus. Lake water on a clear day down by the house on Table Rock.

Death happens from the feet up, a doctor said earlier, tracing the mottled skin of Dad's arches. Death creeps up his body the way I coax mine to sleep, telling feet that they are heavy, are sinking, are bricks, are sagging the mattress toward the floor: calves, knees, thighs, torso, heart, heavy, sagging.

I stop a nurse in the hall. She checks her chart.

Everything's down, she says.

Temperature, pulse, blood pressure, his body shutting down.

What will I tell Sophie about the grandpa she won't remember? I hold my breath again in the long, long space after Dad's outbreath. I lean forward, waiting.

Should I call someone?

Dad drags in air again.

One, two, three, green. His grass before his illness, hard sour gooseberries he made into pies, beans and spinach from his garden.

Nine, ten, eleven, green: a gravestone's rash of moss, leaves on trees he planted years ago, branches the size of my number two pencils.

Green: leaves that shade the yard, that rustle together like these last breaths, tonight, far away, rustling in the wind.

Six hours after nurses remove the oxygen and detach the pump, I log on to my e-mail to get the phone number where Sara is staying. Instead I find a note from my colleague Benjy about why he will oppose my tenure, why I should look for a job elsewhere. Indeed, I have energetically tackled many projects and inspired many students, but he finds my timing for protesting policies and making proposals inappropriate. In the long run, he does not think I will make the necessary sacrifices for the institution.

"Now that you have your beautiful Sophie, how will your time be divided?" he writes.

&

My house is strewn with toys, just as I left it during my abrupt departure two weeks ago. There is still an indentation in the mattress where I sat drying my hair the morning my mom called. Sophie's heavy-lidded eyes peer around at the rooms as we pass through. They all seem strange to me. In my closet, there's a Christmas ornament I bought Dad in China. In my freezer is his unfinished carton of banana ice cream, coated with little ice crystals.

Last week, preparing to go to the funeral home, my six-year-old niece was giddy. "We're going to go see Grandpa," I heard her say.

"Sid?" I said cautiously. Jeff and I had wanted a closed casket, but we yielded to Bob's desire for an open one. Mom got out the suit Dad had been saving for my stepgrandma's funeral and sent it to the mortuary for him to be buried in. "Sid, you know, Grandpa's body will be in a box, but it won't be him," I said. "His spirit isn't there anymore."

Sidney looked confused. "You mean his bones will be in a box?"

I nodded.

"His skin will be in a box?"

"Yes," I said, feeling cruel.

What could I say to Sidney, dismantling her Grandpa in her imagination? How could I erase this image of a cardboard box piled with body parts? How do you explain death to a six-year-old?

Now, back in South Carolina, I remember when I was little, how when we used to come home from Dairy Queen or the grocery store, Dad would say, "I wonder who lives here." We crept up to the front door like intruders on our own lives, space aliens or anthropologists from the future examining the house for clues into the lives of foreigners.

"It looks like they eat this yellow meat," Dad would say, offering me a banana to taste. "Hey, look, when you flip this switch, it's daytime inside."

I giggled at Dad's observations, feeling a little thrill at each discovery. Tiptoeing behind him, I was terrified of getting caught by the house's real inhabitants, forgetting, briefly, that we were they.

Now, as I carry Sophie up the stairs and start her bathwater, she gazes around in wonder. She strokes the shower curtain and erupts with a little shriek of joy at the sight of her bath toys. When I lower her into her crib, she fondly touches each familiar stuffed animal before she closes her eyes and drops off.

I stand there watching her. Not long ago I paused in a hospital room from folding blankets and gathering pillows, slippers, keys, and wallets. I edged closer to my dad's body, listening hard. His stomach growled. I searched for an emergency button, opened my mouth to call someone. But I knew the sound didn't mean he was still alive. And so I stood and looked

at his slack, upturned hands, waiting for some twitch, some flicker of life.
Those hands with their once-firm grip, those fingers with their firecrack-
er snap. Those hands that used to tremble a little with age, those hands
that once caught a bird in them.

I remember this now, and how when he threw that bird out the door,
for a second it seemed borne by the momentum of his toss. How it sailed
for just a second and then its wings took over, rising into their own memory of flight.

Pennsylvania

8

In September, Floyd, a hurricane the size of Texas, makes its way up the coast. Former students who live in Charleston arrive in the upstate after twelve hours on the highway; it's normally a three-hour drive. The glut of traffic under mandatory evacuation finally forces the state to convert the four-lane highway into a one-way exit from Charleston. Return is, for the moment, impossible.

In the largest peacetime evacuation in U.S. history, thirty-eight thousand people move into shelters. My colleagues and students with Charleston ties are all resigned to losing their homes.

Once, recently, my friend Cindy in Arkansas asked if we'd had much rain in South Carolina during the summer, and I realized I had no idea. I could tell her the days my baby had had a fever. I knew it had often been very hot; I remembered sluggishness and Sophie's wet hair. The hospital, I recall, was freezing cold, requiring sweatpants and blankets. But the weather? I have little memory.

So with a bang, Hurricane Floyd brings me back to awareness of the outdoors. With a vague feeling that as a mom I should make more preparations for storms, I wheel Sophie around the grocery store. There's a cart jam in the canned goods aisle, clusters of people everywhere discussing weather predictions and reminiscing about Hurricane Hugo. The white bread and bottled water shelves have been picked clean. I can't think of a single thing to buy that will fortify me against disaster, so I take Sophie home and then pile important papers in the downstairs closet.

All evening, the air blows cool and moist. The sounds of sirens and trains carry farther. Slugs slip in under the kitchen door, always the sign of an impending storm. Sophie and I are nodding off by eight. Sometime in the night, Floyd loses power and heads north, not touching down till somewhere in North Carolina.

My life, so recently tumbling by, has screeched to a standstill. Suddenly, I'm noticing details. I stare in awe at the turrets and columns and gables of the Victorian houses all along Laurens's Main Street, where I push the stroller while Sophie kicks her legs and yells "hi" and "bye bye" to everyone we pass. I'm mesmerized by all of the ordinary life, people pushing lawn mowers and blowing grass off their sidewalks, speed walking up and down the street, waving hoses in high arcs to spray flowers. I maneuver the stroller around a splintered tree trunk. Why did that tree fall? When? Was there a storm?

Jody wrote me last week. She has started the paperwork to adopt a Chinese baby. I'm noticing leaves again, the way light filters through and shadows the sidewalk with their shifting shapes. Grief still froths up regularly like carbonation but eventually shrinks again to something manageable, just a little bit tingly, a little bit painful, in the back of the throat. I know from experience that gradually it goes flat. And eventually, it goes. I know that.

We walk to the playground of the school where Sophie will start kindergarten if we are here in a few years. The thought gives me that cramped, confined feeling I have whenever I picture a future in South Carolina. I can't envision Sophie attending the little brick school with all its add-on trailer classrooms. Covered with red dirt, Sophie runs across the grassy field while I contemplate the bald patches under the swings and jungle gym, the hundreds of overlapping sneaker prints in the dirt, an abandoned Chapstick case. Sophie's a pink speck in the distance. I dash after her.

I collect up the details I would have told my dad, imagine the video footage I would have shot for him. *Dad,* I think, *Remember how you used to complain that I always had my nose stuck in a book? Sophie has learned from me to carry a book with her everywhere. Yesterday on her evening stroll she was paging through Anna Quindlen's* How Reading Changed My Life. *As we entered the bank this afternoon, I discovered that the book tucked under her arm was* H Is for Homicide. *Every day in the car she only settles down and puts up with the twenty-minute drive when I recite the entire texts of* Chicka Chicka ABC *and* But Not the Hippopotamus.

If you were still alive, Dad, I'd get out the camcorder again. I'd reread the directions, recharge the batteries, rewind to the part you shot, start the camera again, make these tapes to send you: Sophie strolling across the living room, arm looped through the handles of a Pooh gift sack she found in her closet, loading it up with things to take to day care—a few diapers, some Cheerios, a strawberry, a brown crayon, some junk mail. Sophie throwing bread pans onto the floor just because she likes the noise. Sophie bouncing to Ozzy Osbourne as he sings a duet with Miss Piggy.

Sophie, pulling her toy drawer over to use as a step up to the coffee table. How she crawls across it, cautious, acclimating herself to this new height, then stands. With the amazement and self-importance of an explorer atop Everest or an astronaut stepping onto the moon, she performs her equivalent to a pumping fist, a planted flag: she laughs. Warbles with laughter, delight bubbling up as she walks back and forth across the table.

And then, the next day, she stares longingly at the coffee table, the memory of her conquest flickering across her face, followed by puzzlement: she can't remember how she did it. She flings a leg up onto the table then cries, unable to repeat her feat.

The night of the winter solstice, the moon is huge and full above the apartment complex's clubhouse, which drips with lights shaped like icicles, the closest to the real thing we'll get around here. Wreaths decorate the fronts of trucks. Someone has hung one on the dumpster. As I slip out to get the laundry, I regret not being more festive, not putting up a Christmas tree or stockings for Sophie.

Today the moon appears 14 percent larger than usual. According to an e-mail Cindy forwards, our ancestors witnessed this phenomenon 133 years ago; our descendants will witness it again in another hundred years. It is so bright tonight that in some places, headlights are unnecessary.

All fall I've felt like I was dashing through a downpour, trying to find the dry spaces between raindrops—an hour here and there during nap time, after bedtime, or between classes and grading and meetings to write job applications, work on freelance articles, do an editing job, put together a synopsis of my novel, and revise sections. I miss unstructured time. I miss goofing off. Every minute of every day is tightly scheduled. It's shocking sometimes to realize that I'm not just babysitting. No one is going to show up to pick up the baby. Nor will any relatives or friends drop in to pinch-hit.

I fantasize about one tranquil day: a new novel, a comfortable chair, a short doze, sunlight filtered through the window prism and swimming across the floor, a new Paul Simon or Alison Krauss CD playing. What I get instead is tuna in the baby's eyebrows, a snowstorm of snotty Kleenex on the carpet, and endless repetitions of "The Teddy Bears' Picnic" and "The Twelve Dogs of Christmas." Instead I try to distract Sophie from sticking her head through the blind slats, nudging a glass of Coke across the kitchen table to see what will happen if it goes over the edge, or removing the stereo cabinet shelves and chewing on the tiny brackets that hold them up.

I am so tired. Sara and I start so many e-mails with this complaint, we eventually abbreviate it: IAST. I watch Sophie in the bathtub. When I drain the water, she's astonished at the way her toys float away. She strains after her duck, fish, and waterwheel; she grabs fistfuls of water that slip between her fingers. The water gurgles away while she keeps scooping up handfuls, trying to grip what won't be held. I watch her hands, the tremor that seizes them before it runs through her whole body. I'm so tired I can't manage to leap to my feet; instead, I wonder idly whether I should take her to the emergency room, the way she is trembling like someone old. Maybe this is the beginning of some terrible disease.

And then I realize that she's cold. She normally runs so hot, I've never seen her shiver.

This is how tired I am. IAST.

It's almost Christmas, and soon we will leave for a sad holiday in Missouri without my dad. Soon we will go to the convention where I have job interviews. It's almost Christmas, and a month ago, Sara wrote to me that she was sitting in her apartment with an enormous case of donor specimen packed in liquid nitrogen, waiting to ovulate. Now, after one insemination, she's pregnant.

Dad, Sophie knows sixteen words now. You should hear her when she's been to the cow pasture down the street from her day care. She comes home making a sound deep in her throat that sounds nothing like "moo" and everything like a real cow.

Change hurtles by, even though here in South Carolina the grass stays green. The leaves lining the edges of the street, now crumbled to dust, and the browned pine needles coating the ground are the only signs that autumn has passed into winter.

Dad, now she knows thirty words. You would get such a kick out of this explosion of language. She calls the tissue box the nose box, *the belt that holds up her pants her* seat belt, *the cow slippers Jody sent her her* moo shoes.

Every day the kitchen floor I used to mop once a month is sticky. Every other day the trash overflows the cans, the laundry spills out of the basket. When I move the couch, the floor underneath is littered with board books, crayons, Legos, and small stuffed animals. I stare with yearning at a picture in a mail-order catalog, a clean, empty nightstand containing nothing but a clock, a book, and a pair of reading glasses. I want that nightstand. I want the clean, simple life it represents. My own nightstand is a jumble of Kleenex, cold medicines, books, papers to be graded, my manuscript, a manuscript I'm editing. I fall into a sleep too crammed with dreams, and wake in the night with an urgent, irrational need to take stock of my life and all the items on my nightstand. "A comb and a brush and a bowl full of mush!" I think, and go back to sleep.

In the spring, the neighbor's loud music wakes me nightly and the decisions I am trying to make about our future keep me up. Whenever I left for a job interview at the convention, Sophie threw herself against the hotel door and screamed while Mom stared blankly into space on the other side of the room; I walked away each day to the thuds of Sophie's body slamming into wood. I didn't know how I would ever travel to campus interviews, and so I withdrew from the job market.

In the meantime, several colleagues went to bat for me with the dean, and then Benjy did an about-face and told me that he was now in favor of my tenure. Three colleagues told me that it was possible I'd not only receive tenure and a promotion, but that I'd be appointed department chair. The thought of more duties right now makes me weary; the unpredictability of my changes in status makes me even wearier. I say nothing.

I don't want to spend my life here, but for the short-term, my options are few. And for the first time in my life, I can't just make the decision that's best for me. I'm trying to figure out what's right for Sophie. I can't imagine totally uprooting her right now. I want to give her continuity. I want to surround her with people who will remember her.

My neighbor's bass rattles the walls whenever Sophie goes down for a nap and his cigarette butts litter my yard. If Mom comes to visit, she won't be able to climb the stairs. I want to live in a place with sidewalks. I want time to mop the kitchen floor in the morning before work. I want to be able to go home for lunch. But would it be foolish to try to move right now?

I win a national award that becomes the lead story on my college's website for months. The dean writes me a glowing letter that praises all of the work I've done over the last year and urges me to go up for early tenure.

I keep thinking about the hippopotamus in Sophie's Sandra Boynton book. All the other animals keep having fun together, "but not the hippopotamus," who is always left out. But then, at the end,

The animal pack comes scurrying back
And says, "Hey! Come join the lot of us!"
But she just doesn't know. Should she stay? Should she go?

Whenever I come to the last page, there's a lump in my throat: *But YES the hippopotamus!* The hippopotamus goes scurrying away with the rest of the animals. Maybe I too will dance off manically with my colleagues if I just resign myself to staying here.

If anyone finds out that my literary points of reference are currently illustrated board books, I will be denied tenure for sure.

I buy a house. I start assembling my tenure file. I make my first big stab at doing the right thing for my child, and my last little stab at being the daughter I've always imagined that my parents wanted, the kind who could succeed at a church-connected school.

Dad would approve of my house. It has pine floors and built-in bookshelves and two fireplaces. It's a two-minute drive to my office, a one-minute drive to Sophie's day care. Our yard is a small park, shaded by crepe myrtles and pecan and fig trees, bordered by beds of roses, honeysuckle, holly, and azaleas, sidewalks lined with liriope. All of this is ours, and the little bed of wood chips, and the gravel in the driveway. I hang a hummingbird feeder, wind chimes, and a porch swing. There are sidewalks all the way to the park and the duck pond, so I buy a wagon for Sophie's second birthday. I can't believe I have all of this space after years of flimsy apartments, tiny fenced patio spaces, and doors leading out to parking lots. I wish I could ask Dad's advice about fertilizer and paint and how to kill weeds. In the late summer I open all the windows that aren't nailed shut and listen to the trains and the crickets and the unripe figs falling onto the shed roof.

Mom wants to send me her thirty-two place settings of Desert Rose Franciscanware now that I am settled, a mom, and a homeowner. For years, visiting the homes of colleagues, I've wondered at their heavy dark antique tables, their china cabinets and buffets and enormous glass-fronted bookshelves and the mysterious confidence in permanence it must take to acquire so much weight in furniture. My own stuff seemed so comparatively light and unstable, my grad school pressed-board shelves and wobbly chairs, my old couches whose gapes in the cushions my mom had repaired with huge dental-floss stitches. It's not that I don't covet beautiful, heavy things. It's just that I've always been impatient with burdens, wanting to travel light, believing I could shed the past the way my trees relinquish all their leaves in the fall.

Not yet, I tell Mom. Don't send the dishes yet.

Dad, whenever I leave Sophie at day care or with a babysitter, she has to give me a hug, a kiss, and a push. All the other kids are demanding to push their mommies out the door, now, too. She is so much bigger and more verbal than the last time you saw her.

Videos I wish I could shoot for you: Sophie wandering around the house singing "Lolly lolly lolly get your adverbs here."

Sophie pursing her lips and leaning over to kiss her classroom's pet frog, squealing when it jumps, and telling me over and over, dreamily all evening, "I like that frog, Mommy."

Sophie, seeing Judy Garland singing "Somewhere over the Rainbow," throwing her arms out for months afterward and bellowing, "Why?"

Sophie's favorite outfit: a sleeveless pink dress with a kitty on it, always worn with hot pink rain boots.

In September, Mom has the first of ten or twelve small strokes over the next year. Suddenly, she can't pronounce words. They come out a jumble of strange sounds. On the way to the emergency room, Mom asks Aunt Arlene for the names of her grandchildren. Mom pulls a scrap of paper from her purse and takes notes: Sidney. Treven. Megan. Sophie.

My brother Jeff drives down from Ohio with boxes of stuff sent by Mom. Disintegrating dolls from my childhood, yellowed birthday cards, lots of framed pictures of myself, old broken watches, some dried up Play-Doh in plastic bags.

I rake the yard, all the leaves like shriveled husks, and Sophie scatters the piles. All over the neighborhood, rakes rasp. Sometimes I watch Sophie leaping through the leaves and think, "Where did this Chinese baby come from?" Her terrible twos are downright terrible at times, so much so that a man I briefly date thinks maybe I need to seek family counseling, though he readily admits that he has never been around two-year-olds. He seems to think that he and she are in a competition for my attention, and soon I let the relationship go without much regret. I watch Sophie throw tantrums and muse at how ever-more-willingly enslaved I am.

We walk, following the tractor path through the pasture, all of the cows turning to look at us with big dumb eyes, swishing their tails, lowering their heads to scratch them on fence slats and knocking off herds of flies in the process. Sophie and I take turns shouting, "How now brown cow!"

My routine has magically started to click. I sleep enough, write every day, keep the house presentable, do my job, read books, and play with Sophie. And yet I'm stressed out all the time, especially since the hire of a new composition specialist, a black Trinidad-born woman. Benjy had initially voted against offering her the job, mostly because her voice, like mine, was in a register he had more trouble hearing. "Beyond her exotic appearance and lilting voice, she's essentially empty," he declared in a department meeting.

To my surprise, the rest of the department overrode him and voted to hire her. I was heartened by this—until she arrived on campus. Repeatedly, this very pleasant woman with dreadlocks has been scolded and harassed by administrators and colleagues for seeming "inaccessible" and "hostile" and for teaching according to her expertise rather than adhering to the outdated departmental policies I have spent years fighting against.

I spend a day drawing up, using the most diplomatic tone I can manage, a proposal for grading guidelines that will bridge the gaps between the four decades of training represented by our department. All of my colleagues compliment the proposal. Then, one by one, all of them say that they will not support it. Two untenured colleagues yell at me for making waves.

My blood pressure is way up, so much that I talk to my doctor about medication for hypertension. I buy teas with names like Stress Buster and Tension Tamer. I imagine that tenure will at least give me enough security to speak up without fearing repercussions. But as Sophie and I settle into a comfortable routine that allows me time to do my job and write and still play with her, I'm struggling against the sneaking suspicion that tenure means quiet collusion with intolerance and tyranny, and that beyond tenure lies a stiflingly complacent life without real challenges.

Sophie is bilingual. She says "Mom" and "Mama" interchangeably. She plays both "Peekaboo" and "Peepeye." When her Pooh pops out of a barrel, she says "Hi, Pooh," with a distinctively southern accent. I push the button that releases Pooh over and over, just so I can hear her southern drawl. I laugh hysterically the first time she says "Yes, Ma'am" to me and then I chastise myself: if we're going to live in the South, I should be encouraging her southern manners. At dinner she demands that we say a blessing, like they do at her day care.

What has most struck me about watching her development is how much she becomes more herself all the time, how the baby I met a year and a half ago flowers out into new blooms but remains always the same stubborn, clever child as she turns into a little girl. I'm trying not to mind if she becomes a little southern girl, just as long as she keeps her ferocious determination and her sly wit.

In early December, Sara brings her new son, Isaac, for a visit. I'm amazed at the way I can cup his fuzzy blond head in my hand. He's a mellow baby, one with an intense ability to focus, and I imagine the little boy he will become.

I give Sara a tour of the house. Compared to her small, expensive apartment in the D.C. suburbs, my little house seems spacious and lavish. Through her eyes, I am reminded that it's a wonderful house and that I'm lucky; through my dissatisfaction and restlessness, I always know that I am fortunate, but it's good to be reminded as Sara admires the blue and black kitchen that is like something from a magazine and the cozy den behind it that used to be a porch.

On our way outside, I pull mail from the box, and see, in the corner of a long envelope, the college president's return address. Catalogs and credit card offers scatter across the porch. My hands no longer seem to belong to me, shaking violently, out of my control, as if I'm in one of those dreams where I'm trying and trying to get my shoes on before I miss the bus, or dial the phone in an emergency, but I keep making mistakes, can't seem to perform the most simple acts. I call out to Sara but she's in the driveway, securing Isaac in the car seat, and she doesn't hear me. My finger slices the envelope jaggedly. Somehow I unfold the letter. Words march like stern soldiers across the page: *You will not be tenured or promoted.*

ℱℑ

I don't open the drapes for weeks. Students bring me presents, write letters protesting the decision, fix us a spaghetti dinner, and show up at the door with some breakfast concoction that involves an egg called Toad in a Hole. Administrators refuse to talk to me. Most of the colleagues I thought were my friends never call.

"They think you're a lesbian," one of my friends elsewhere announces.

"They think you're rejecting men because you're raising a child alone," another friend says.

A colleague has been granted tenure only after extensive discussion of whether she is a good mother. "Maybe they think you're publishing too much to be a good mother," another friend theorizes.

I want to believe that no employer would terminate a contract over such conjectures, but I've lived here long enough to know that mine might. Still, I know that my biggest crime was that I failed to remain silent and obedient, that I didn't passively give in to orders and policies that troubled me.

"Mama's sad," Sophie keeps saying, and takes to diapering all the stuffed animals in her crib. Before climbing out of the bathtub, she tucks her rubber duck into a makeshift bed under a washcloth.

For six weeks I struggle with anxiety so intense I imagine myself walking in front of a speeding truck. I'm not suicidal. I just want the terror to go away.

And then, here is this little Chinese girl twirling across the den, this little girl who keeps growing and changing and needing things, so I have to rise up out of my paralysis and feed her and read her books and give her baths. She leaps into my customary place on the couch and lies there, giggling, thwarting my attempt to return. She pulls on my black tights, like a body stocking on her, and wobbles around the house. I wonder if I would have adopted her if I'd known that in two years' time I would lose my dad, watch my mom descend into illness and depression, and lose my job. The answer is no. I wouldn't have.

I'm so stunned at this realization, I can't swallow. I can't breathe.

I'd have never adopted her if I'd known how alone I'd be, alternating now between enervating panics and surges of adrenaline, able to talk only to a few old friends, marooned on my own separate island. The shipwreck is there, underneath the water, and eventually I'll have to dive in to see what I can recover. At the end of dopey movies, in the middle of the night, I wake with shock at how wrecked I feel.

Then, every day, I pull myself together to take care of my baby. The unwavering power of my love and gratitude never stops amazing me. The job I'm leaving seems so trivial next to the profound presence of this child. Her loss is the only thing I could not bear.

The summer I left Nebraska, trains thundered endlessly through Lincoln, Burlington Northern and Amtrak whistling out their primitive plaintive yearning. Often I'd get stuck waiting for trains that rumbled the ground underneath my car while drivers around me gunned impatiently. I counted the train cars, rust-colored, silver, green, blue, more weathered-looking than in comic strips and children's cartoons but still colorful. The caboose always trailed, the guardrails lifted, and all the automobiles surged forward like horses out of a gate.

I used to love those trains. I'd wake at night and imagine my griefs hopping aboard them like children old enough to travel alone. They came back to me tough and independent, a little easier to live alongside.

Now, my last spring in South Carolina, trains barrel along at night, but I do not lie awake listening longingly or feeling philosophical. Instead I hold my breath, waiting for Sophie's cry to curl out from beneath the clatter of rails, the wail of whistles.

"I scared of trains," she says, pointing at the window with a trembling finger.

I attack her fear with zeal because this is a fear that can be attacked. We read books about freight trains with pages that slide back to reveal the cows and chickens and coal and vegetables inside the cars. We read about the little engine that could. We trace the movements of a miniature train that circles on tracks near the ceiling of the Bilo store. When we are stopped by trains she whimpers but leans forward, caught up by her awe and fascination and fear as the train rattles by, every car the same gray, long since having lost their paint. And now there are no cabooses to signal the end.

Trains have lost their luster. They no longer feel like freedom to me, or maybe that kind of freedom is something I no longer crave. If Sophie cries, if I wake, I fret over my lost sleep and feel the weight of all my griefs that I cannot send away. I no longer trust them to cycle back to me soothed. Now there is too much freight.

But when I finally dig beneath my terror of the future to start the long excavation of my own wreckage, what I find surprises me. Certainly doubt, fear, a loss of trust. But none of the insecurities I expected to rear up, no floundering in my old anxieties about not being smart enough or a good enough mother. Mysteriously, I have shucked an old husk like the cicadas in my parents' yard that left behind a litter of dry brown shells. What I have left is a calm certainty that I've followed a conscience my parents might never have fully understood, even though they're the ones who taught me to stand up for what I believed. The dozens of mistakes I've made have not been driven by stupidity but by a wisdom beyond me that wouldn't allow my complicity in maintaining a world I don't want my daughter to inherit.

When people told me that being a single mom would be hard, they didn't have a clue what they were talking about, and neither did I. How easy and inevitable it would be in one way, how truly, terribly hard in another. But when I think back on all my doubts about adopting Sophie, I know that she is the only thing I am sure about.

I'm floored by the improbability of her, the sheer implausibility that she managed to slip through the cracks into my life. Underneath my desperation about our future, I glimpse relief and wonder. I'm puzzled by and beholden to the mysterious force that led me to her: what some people call intuition, or the internal compass, or premonition, or the still small voice of God, that thin splinter of knowledge that there was a baby somewhere in the world who needed me. Whom I, too, needed.

Sophie and I read *A Mother for Choco* every night before bed. One night she asks, "But why didn't Choco already have a mommy?"

I offer her a garbled explanation about how sometimes babies have mommies that can't take care of them, so then another mommy gets to be their mommy.

"You know, you had a first mommy before me," I say.

Sophie claps her hand over my mouth. She doesn't want to hear it, not right now.

I've been planning these conversations long before I knew her, how I will tell her the story of her past. So I am startled by my own reaction, how jolted I am at saying those words aloud, how relieved I am when she stops me. I've reached a point where it takes a leap of imagination to fully realize that there was a mommy before me. I think of this woman often, the woman who had to give up the one thing I could not stand to lose, but in my heart I have transformed into Sophie's first and only mommy.

It's March and we walk again. By an act of Congress, Sophie, like other children adopted overseas, is now a U.S. citizen. Jody will be home soon with her new baby, Josie. Oddly, after four and a half years of building, my blood pressure drops to normal without benefit of medication.

As Sophie and I head outside, I don't know whether it's overcast or dusk or both. The air is warm but with an undercurrent of chill, like the way you feel the presence of pain hidden under the blankness of aspirin. We walk past the cows and pigs to the rose garden, our old Saturday walk. The daffodils and crepe myrtles bloomed weeks ago, and now the garden near Sophie's school is bright with roses. After nine interview requests and a clinging baby as I left her with friends to go to four of them, I turned down the rest and signed a contract. We are moving to the mountains of northwestern Pennsylvania, where I imagine us sipping hot cocoa as we watch snow fall past an upstairs window. I'm taking things one step at a time. Otherwise, I'm overwhelmed at the prospect of selling my house, buying another one, finding a day care, and moving us both. One step at a time, it will all happen, and on our way in my car crammed with blankets and clothes and cleaning supplies, we will make our last stop in Greenville to have dinner with my old adoption support group and their kids. We've drifted in separate directions, our beliefs so different, but we still feel tender toward each other's children, the ones that, together, we waited so long for.

At the park, large women with booming voices yell at small children with juice-stained mouths. The sky is the delicate blue of a robin's shell, the wind hearty and brisk. All morning, it clattered my stove fan. Trees dive-bomb pinecones on us and leaves skitter up behind us like wild puppies. The pines crowd together, trunks long thin poles crowned by needles. In our yard, the hyacinths are blooming, and there's a circle of purple flowers around the crepe myrtles. I don't know the flowers' name.

Dad, if you were alive, you'd tell me the names of things. If I'd lived here long enough, maybe I would have learned them anyway.

Sophie's tired. She tugs at my hand and hops back into the wagon. As I pull her toward home, my memory flashes, the smell of evening air, the clatter of wagon wheels bringing back walks when I was three, my dad pulling me over sidewalks to the grocery store. I can feel this, what it was like to be in the wagon bumping over the sidewalk cracks, but I cannot quite picture it: the only images that come to mind are the house on Morris Street, the tin box on the porch where a man delivered bottles of cold milk each morning, the sound of an ice cream truck, tinkling nickelodeon music loud outside the door then fading into the distance.

From her crib, Sophie pulls picture books off her shelf and flips through them till she falls asleep. I watch her sleeping on the heap of books, the corner of one grazing her cheek, another one clutched in her fist. When I go to bed, I dream I am blowing up a balloon for her, but the air keeps escaping, my own breath breathing back at me, the balloon deflating. Then I blow again into the shapeless piece of rubber and watch it grow, taking on the shape it would have anyway.

Somehow in my dream I know that raising a child is like this, that living a life is like this, with false starts but still all there, waiting to take shape. All you can give is your breath.

About the Author

Nancy McCabe's creative nonfiction has won a Pushcart Prize and been listed in *Best American Essays* twice. She is the author of *After the Flashlight Man: A Memoir of Awakening* and the Assistant Professor of Writing and Director of Writing Programs at the University of Pittsburgh in Bradford.

Photo by Bill McCabe